"אל אוזר לאגׁ, בקׁפׁוֹבׁ! אוג חׁ'ק בׁטׁ אוֹג ה בׁ'ק חׁ אוֹזׁ בׁ"

Micah Gentin
2021

P9-DHD-233

And From There You Shall Seek

MeOtzar HoRav SERIES:
SELECTED WRITINGS OF
RABBI JOSEPH B. SOLOVEITCHIK

The MeOtzar HoRav *series has been made possible by a
generous grant from Ruth and Irwin Shapiro.*

The publication of this volume has been enabled
by a grant from the Brickman family
in memory of their father
הרב שמואל צבי בן יוסף הלוי
הולך תמים ופעל צדק ודבר אמת בלבבו

ובקשתם משם

And From There You Shall Seek

Rabbi Joseph B. Soloveitchik

Translated from the Hebrew by
Naomi Goldblum

Published for
THE TORAS HORAV FOUNDATION
by Ktav Publishing House

And From There You Shall Seek
Rabbi Joseph B. Soloveitchik
Translated from the Hebrew by Naomi Goldblum

© 2008 TORAS HORAV FOUNDATION

Library of Congress Cataloging-in-Publication Data

Soloveitchik, Joseph Dov.
[U-vikashtem mi-sham. English]
And from there you shall seek / Joseph B. Soloveitchik
translated from the Hebrew by Naomi Goldblum.
    p. cm.
"Published for The Toras HoRav Foundation by Ktav Publishing House, Inc."
Includes bibliographical references and index.
ISBN 978-0-88125-934-6
1. God (Judaism) 2. Providence and government of God – Judaism. 3. Judaism –
Doctrines. 4. Spiritual life – Judaism. I. Title.
    BM610.S57513 2008
    296.3'11 – dc22

2008050761

Printing year: 2021

ISBN 978-0-88125-934-6

Published for
THE TORAS HORAV FOUNDATION
by **KTAV PUBLISHING HOUSE**
527 Empire Blvd., Brooklyn, NY 11225

Website: www.ktav.com
Email: orders@ktav.com
ph: (718)972-5449 / Fax: (718)972-6307

Typeset in Minion by KPS

MeOtzar HoRav SERIES:
SELECTED WRITINGS OF RABBI JOSEPH B. SOLOVEITCHIK
Editorial-Publication Board
David Shatz, Series Editor
Joel B. Wolowelsky, Associate Editor
Reuven Ziegler, Director of Research

🪶 Table of Contents

And From There You Shall Seek

‌ Preface

R abbi Joseph B. Soloveitchik *zt"l* (1903–1993) was one of the outstanding talmudists of the twentieth century and in addition one of its most creative and seminal Jewish thinkers. His writings brought Jewish thought and law to bear on the interpretation and assessment of the modern experience. Rabbi Soloveitchik built bridges between Judaism and the modern world while vigorously upholding the integrity and autonomy of the Jew's faith commitment, in particular the commitment to a life governed by Halakhah, Jewish law.

For over four decades, Rabbi Soloveitchik gave the senior *shi'ur* (class in Talmud) at the Rabbi Isaac Elchanan Theological Seminary (RIETS), affiliated with Yeshiva University. Generations of rabbinical students were taught and inspired by him, among them many of the future leaders of all areas of Jewish communal life. He was the halakhic authority and spiritual leader of the Rabbinical Council of America, founded the Maimonides School in Boston, and also served as the chief rabbinic figure in that city (commuting weekly between there and New York). He contributed vitally to the dynamic resurgence of Orthodox Judaism in America.

This volume brings to the English-speaking community a translation of Rabbi Soloveitchik's classic work, "*U-Vikkashtem mi-Sham*." We trust that the essay's characteristic intellectual sweep and energizing passion will enrich new generations of readers.

David Shatz
Joel B. Wolowelsky
Reuven Ziegler

ஐ Introduction

David Shatz and Reuven Ziegler

The present volume is a translation of Rabbi Joseph B. Soloveitchik's powerful and wide-ranging Hebrew essay "*U-Vikkashtem mi-Sham*." Anecdotal evidence suggests that it occupied a central and especially important place in its author's mind, and indeed no analysis of Rabbi Soloveitchik's understanding of religious experience and consciousness – his religious phenomenology – can be complete without taking account of and grappling with this rich and complex work. Despite its importance – or perhaps because of it – whereas Rabbi Soloveitchik drafted this essay in the 1940's, shortly after completing his first major philosophical work, "*Ish ha-Halakhah*,"[1] "*U-Vikkashtem mi-Sham*" did not appear in print until 1978, when the Rav published it in the rabbinic journal *Hadarom*.

In the three decades he took to publish the essay, the Rav experimented with various titles. In its early stage it was called "*Ish ha-Elokim*," "The Man of God"; in a 1963 letter to the noted rabbinic scholar Dr. Samuel K. Mirsky,[2] the Rav refers to it as "*Halakhah Geluyah ve-Ahavah Mesuteret*," "Overt Halakhah and Covert Love," the same title as the final version's first section; then, in the published version, he opted for the name "*U-Vikkashtem mi-Sham*," "And From There You Shall Seek," a title that draws on a verse in Deuteronomy (4:29): "And from there you shall seek the Lord your God, and you will find Him if only you seek Him with all your heart and all your soul."

The present translation fills a need that has been acutely felt ever since the original appeared in 1978. The Rav's rich and beautiful Hebrew style, ranging as it does from soaring poetry to halakhic analysis to rigorous philosophical exposition, and incorporating creative uses of biblical, rabbinic and philosophical allusions, challenges and perhaps frustrates even readers who are fluent in Hebrew. Thanks to the labors of Naomi Goldblum, we have before us now, in a form accessible to a broad audience, the essay that the Rav believed "surpasses [*Ish ha-Halakhah*] in content and form."[3]

Following the pattern of previous volumes in the *MeOtzar HoRav* series, we shall here offer the reader an exposition of the work. In the concluding part of this essay, we shall briefly examine the relationship between *And From There You Shall Seek* and *Halakhic Man*.

THE DIALECTIC OF THE SONG OF SONGS

As noted above, the title *And From There You Shall Seek* is drawn from Deuteronomy 4:29. There the Jewish people are told that while in exile, an exile that is due to their sins, they will sin still more and will worship idols. Nonetheless: "And from there you shall seek the Lord your God, and you will find Him if only you seek Him with all your heart and all your soul."

The words of this verse provide a crisp, pointed statement of the essay's main theme: the quest for God.[4] The human being experiences, to quote the letter to Dr. Mirsky, the "obligation and... desire to run toward the Holy One, Blessed Be He."

The "plot" of searching and seeking is presented right at the beginning of the essay via a lyrical exposition of the Song of Songs. This biblical book presents us with a narrative concerning two lovers, and was interpreted by Jewish tradition either as an allegory for the relationship between God and the people Israel or (as in

Maimonides, Laws of Repentance 10:3) that between God and the individual. (Tradition also has it that precisely because of its depiction of the divine-human encounter, Rabbi Akiva declared the Song of Songs to be, of all biblical books, the "holiest of the holy.") Rabbi Soloveitchik's understanding of the love story follows the tradition of allegory – indeed, in a footnote he insists that the narrative must not be interpreted according to its plain meaning. What he takes the allegory to convey is the love of the created for the Creator and of the Creator for the created.[5]

Rabbi Soloveitchik stresses a strange element within the Song of Songs. The lovers pine for each other, yet repeatedly they fail to take advantage of opportunities to meet. At the very moment he can meet his beloved, the lad retreats and hides among the rocks. Why does he flee? Strange, too, is the behavior of the Shulammite maiden. She asks with her whole being, "Where has my beloved gone?" and depicts herself as "faint with love." Yet when her lover finally arrives and knocks at her door, she is slow to rise and let him in. Then, by the time she leaps off her bed and opens the door, her love raging, her heart expanding – he has left; "my beloved has turned and gone."

What is the significance of a lover who yearns yet hides, a longing bride who conceals herself? The Rav understands this strange "game" in terms of his own allegorical interpretation. The Creator loves the created, but the Creator nevertheless "rests in a hidden place." The created loves the Creator, but nevertheless refuses to open the door. That is to say: God does not reveal Himself fully; and man retreats from God just at the moment of a potential encounter. The rest of the essay seeks to depict how man experiences this dialectical to-and-fro, and how he can overcome it.

THE SEARCH FOR GOD: NATURAL CONSCIOUSNESS

As depicted in the essay, the quest for God begins with the attempt to find God through the exploration of the created world, and culminates, after a long and tortuous journey, in the individual's attaining the state of *devekut*, cleaving to God. Let us map this odyssey step by step, beginning with humanity's attempt to find God by examining every "hidden corner of the natural and spiritual world" (8).

Central to Rabbi Soloveitchik's religious phenomenology (again, his depiction of religious experience and consciousness) is a distinction between two forms of such consciousness, the "natural" and the "revelational." Essentially, the natural consciousness propels the human being (or humanity at large) to find God through the products of human culture. The revelational consciousness results when God reveals Himself to human beings. At its core the essay finds the attempt to find God through culture – for example, through science, which explores "the cosmic drama"; or through the study of spiritual existence; or through the "transcendental experience" – valuable but ultimately inadequate. And yet: just when it seems that the quest for God has simply failed, God reveals Himself to humans, and man comes to possess the revelational consciousness. The Rav believes, however, that both the natural and the revelational modes are essential to religious experience; one without the other is inadequate.

To elaborate, let us first take a partial look at the natural consciousness. To be sure, the activities of human culture are part of the quest for transcendence, a yearning for a realm beyond:

> There is no hidden corner of the natural or spiritual world which man's consciousness, pining for its divine beloved, does not peer into and scrutinize. Human consciousness carefully investigates the buds of transcendence that appear every so often in the spiritual desert...Flesh-and-blood man longs to escape from the straits of the limited, bounded and contingent world and go out into the limitless, independent, wide-open spaces. This search is an act of self-transcendence, which is truly the essence of man's cultural ascent (8).

By examining the natural world, human beings have constructed alleged "proofs" for the existence of a non-contingent being (that is, a being whose existence is not dependent on anything else). But – following a thesis famously advocated by David Hume and Immanuel Kant in the eighteenth century – Rabbi Soloveitchik submits that all such proofs have failed.[6] Furthermore, science has not succeeded in capturing all features of existence. For example, modern physics cannot explain "qualitative reality" – the realm of immediate sensory experience. Science itself, the Rav asserts, has become aware of its limitations and of the "irrational" character of reality. In response, or as if in response, scientists present their theories as abstract mathematical symbolisms; clearly, though, these do not fully capture reality. How, moreover, can cold, abstract reason attain anything but a cold, abstract, impersonal idea – an "achievement" bordering on pantheism? And how, finally, could the study of a finite world reveal infinity?

Perhaps, then, knowledge of God can be based on an immediate awareness achieved by a creature yearning for its Creator; on personal encounter, not logical inference. "The human bond to God is expressed in aspiration, not in casuistry; in yearning, not in clever logical acrobatics" (14). "Taste and see how good is the Lord" (Ps. 34:9). The mystery of creation cannot be captured by science.[7] And yet, even when experience rather than science is the means chosen to complete man's search, the *Shekhinah*, or Divine presence, proves to be both revealed *and* hidden. God eludes His creation; this, partly, because sin precludes man from seeing God everywhere. God *is* everywhere, yet His presence cannot be seen or experienced. He is enveloped, as the Bible says, by a thick cloud.

In the end, a religiosity predicated on cultural consciousness alone leads to spiritual weariness, bankruptcy, and ultimately denial of God.

We can both sum up and expand the matter as follows. Human ontological experience (that is, the human experience of being) manifests itself in two aspects: scientific experience, which is relative, limited, and contingent; and transcendental experience – experience of the infinite within the temporal, bounded and contingent. Whereas the former is expressed in mathematical equations, the latter is expressed, as just indicated, in longings, aspirations, and immediate experience. The world is experienced as "a living, bubbling, effervescent consciousness, burning with the flame of pent-up longing…" (16). Consciousness of a transcendent being is a striving upwards. The ontological consciousness itself involves consciousness of God. Hence the prophets call upon us to search out the secrets of the cosmic process. "The heavens declare the glory of God, the sky proclaims His handiwork," sings King David (Ps. 19:2). The Jew is commanded to utter blessings over all natural phenomena, from sweet-smelling flowers to rainbows, from rising moons to thunder and lightning, from water and bread to the constitution of the human body. In everything, the Jew sees the glory of God. Furthermore, God wants the human being to "fill the earth and subdue it" (Gen. 1:28). But with all that, "Only the combination of scientific reason with the heart that searches and yearns for the living God, can allow man to progress" (44).

REVELATIONAL CONSCIOUSNESS

Human beings can find God in another way as well: through God's initiative, that is to say, revelation. "The voice of my beloved knocks" (Song of Songs 5:2). God brings prophecies to human beings. Interestingly, revelation does not occur as a response to human yearning, but instead arrives suddenly: when the Israelites leave Egypt as slaves still covered in filth and dust, when they sin terribly by creating the Golden Calf, when evil is growing in the world and "a torrent of despair is about to quench all the aspirations of the distressed and yearning soul" (31).

In sum, man searches for God through reason and finds Him in the splendor and glory of the world; we utter benedictions by way of thanksgiving and praise for our existence in a lawful and stable world. But ultimately this mode of finding God fails, due both to its built-in limitations and to human sinfulness. God, however, reveals Himself to man, sometimes out of the black agony of evil and misfortune. Sometimes, "He does not reveal Himself to the rational individual, but to the one who is confused about life, who is bankrupt and has lost track of his world" (33). God reveals Himself through suffering, tragedy, trouble and distress. As biblical examples attest (Adam and Eve, for example, or Jonah), if a creature attempts to run away from God and hide, God overtakes him.

When God reveals Himself, it is not for the sake of helping man realize an intellectual goal. It is for the sake of expressing His will; He wishes to command the human being, to impose discipline and submission. Finding God through His creation is not sufficient because Judaism requires faith in a revelation imposed on people. "The God of Sinai is the God of the Will…The God of creation is the God of the Hidden Intellect…" (35). God's will conquers and subdues man. Man is "absolutely subordinate" (ibid.); his experience is that of compulsion. Man must be ready to fulfill the revelation's imperatives.

Thus, there is a duality in religious experience. Man seeks God, but he is also God's captive. However, the revelational consciousness is closed off from cultural consciousness.

FREEDOM AND COMPULSION

The emotions and orientations of the natural religious consciousness and the revealed religious consciousness differ sharply from each other. A focal example involves freedom. In its "natural" mode, religious consciousness is the consciousness of freedom. Man seeks God out of a thirst for freedom, a desire to be liberated from tyrannical Nature and the travail of life. But "revelational religion lusts for unrestricted control" (43) over the human being; it imposes authority. The commanded human being therefore experiences necessity and subjugation; man's will is preempted, and he accepts the commandments against his will.

The experience of a person who seeks God out of a longing for spiritual freedom is different from that of an individual who recoils when God reveals Himself to him. Sometimes the experience of spontaneous religiosity shoves aside the feeling of obligation and subordination. The result is a religious experience that is cognitive, moral, or aesthetic. An individual who undergoes such experiences rejects authority and chooses only those laws that have a rationale he finds convincing. The result of this freedom is anarchy. Saul of Tarsus (Paul) was wrong in seeing the law as the cause of sin; religiosity lacking the objective-revelational element cannot conquer the beast in man. The Holocaust proves this: "All those who speak of love stood silent and did not protest. Many of them even took part in the extermination of millions of human beings" (55).

MERCY AND JUSTICE, TRUST AND FEAR

The schism between the natural approach, with its yearning for God, and the revelational approach, with its fear of God, is reflected by the difference between two divine attributes, mercy and justice. The individual turns to God because he seeks repose from confusion and aimlessness, refuge from the looming threat of death and nihility. Thus the longing for God is pragmatic. It is born of the biological instinct to continue one's natural existence. At this level, the human being's spiritual aspiration to run towards God emanates from his animal nature. "The love for God embodied in the longing is a selfish love, a love of the reward involved in becoming closer to God: the conquest of man's fear" (48). In this state the human being is oblivious of the commandments.

The preceding description displays God as possessing the attribute of mercy by which the human being is extricated from fear. But God also possesses the attribute of justice. He is a stern and terrifying judge, a punisher who demands self-sacrifice, "utter subordination" (49) and fulfillment of the commandments. Confronted by the attribute of justice that is manifested in revelation, the human being no longer tries to draw near to God's presence, but rather tries to flee from it. This flight is driven by animal panic. Yet, precisely in this flight and fear he serves God. Fear gives rise to the decision to fulfill God's will, if only to avoid the negative consequences of disobedience, and turns into an ongoing revelational awareness.

Although fear at first seems to supplant trust (love), the Rav goes on to portray both as co-existing in dialectical tension, for both trust and fear are necessary components of man's religious consciousness. It is acceptable to look to God for reward and to flee from Him to evade punishment. Such experiences are valuable and significant; Judaism accepts natural man and his simple desire for continued existence.

Since the revelatory experience is imposed from without, man perceives it as being unrelated to his cultural consciousness and unresponsive to his desires and needs. Yet, God wants man to worship Him not only out of sadness and dread, but also out of a spontaneous desire which gladdens the heart: "Serve the Lord out of joy" (Ps. 100:2). Asceticism – withdrawal from the task of improving and settling the world and of tending to physical and psychological needs – results in mediocre religion. As we saw earlier, human beings are commanded to "fill the earth and subdue it" (Gen. 1:28). Natural consciousness "is the wellspring of human feelings of joy and wonder, it gives rise to the stream of happiness and sweetness in life…it tells man to progress, to elevate and improve himself" (56). Human beings must take part in the act of creation.

We now see why both natural and revelational consciousness are necessary. A life based only on natural consciousness evades the authority of religion and is in essence secular; a life based only on revelational consciousness abandons practical action and the real world.

Rabbi Soloveitchik notes, as well, that whereas intellectual religious experience of the sort involved in natural consciousness is an esoteric phenomenon – that is, limited to an elite few who can undertake deep inquiry and investigation (think of scientific inquiry) – revelational faith is exoteric, as the revelation is addressed to all, and its commands can be fulfilled by all, regardless of intellectual capacity and spiritual ability.

Both approaches are necessary. On the one hand, religion belongs to everyone, to the whole community. On the other hand, it must provide the opportunity for the exceptional individual to deepen and broaden his observations of the Divinity. Korah was right in declaring that "All of the community are holy," but wrong in complaining "so why do you raise yourselves above the Lord's congregation?" (Num. 16:3). The exoteric holiness of the community does not distinguish between great and small, but esoteric holiness depends on the greatness and depth of the individual.

YEARNING AND ANNIHILATION

There is a deeper significance to the dichotomy between the natural quest for God and the revelation of God. As Maimonides explains in the very first teaching of his *Mishneh Torah* code, God is the creator of the universe, the cause of all that exists, and He who sustains all existence. A world that exists separate from God is impossible. "There is no existence without God," the Rav states, "and there is no reality without reliance on Him" (62). Because of this, God's existence negates – abrogates – all other existence.

The human being aspires to rise from nothingness to the God who causes everything. But to cleave to the infinite God he must eradicate his finite being, his self. So there is a yearning to come close to God, but also a fear of annihilation. There must be retreat before God, as when the Jewish people had to keep a distance from Mount Sinai at the time of the giving of the Torah, as when a priest must not enter the Holy of Holies where the *Shekhinah* is located, as when a Jew is prohibited from uttering God's name in vain. The Tetragrammaton expresses both the idea of the coming into being of what exists, and the annihilation of what exists.

LOVE AND AWE

The Rav's account of the natural and revelational consciousness stressed the desire for reward and the fear of punishment. What this suggests is that Judaism does not ignore psychosomatic man but rather sees his vital natural eudaemonic (happiness-seeking) yearnings and fears as important for spontaneous religious life. His experience includes bodily and psychic longing and fear. But at a second stage of religious development, the utilitarian desire for reward and fear of punishment – while never entirely superseded – are transformed into the transcendent and mysterious experiences of love and awe.

Love does not expect reward, whereas the earlier stage of biological yearning did. Love takes the form of a free, conscious experience. Man longs for God out of the intellectual study of existence and penetration into the depths of Creation. "Out of the conclusion that 'everything depends on Him for its existence,' he yearns for his Source" (66).

Just as love is different from biological and psychic longing, so too is awe is different from fear. Fear is emotional and instinctual, not intellectual. In extreme forms it leads to neurosis, and a religiosity governed by fear deteriorates into magic. By contrast, "Awe is born of the spirit that soars on high" (67). It stems from assessment of oneself and the Other. Awe begins with knowledge of inferiority and a sense of shame, and ends with spiritual recoil "whose essence is spiritual elevation" (ibid.).

Awe and love are entwined with each other; a lover may experience awe. I love the other for his greatness and majesty, but this valuation leads to the retreat of the lesser one in the face of the greater. As one draws near, one's self-image diminishes. The coexistence of love and awe is also found in the relationship one forms, or should form, with one's parents.

Thus: man runs towards God, but also recoils from Him. As the Rav puts it pointedly: "He runs towards God, for how can man distance himself fom God and live? He retreats from God, for how can man attach himself to God and live?" (69). Hence the pendulum-like movement of the man of God known in Kabbalah as "*ratzo va-shov*," moving back and forth.

Love, then, is the creature's coming closer and cleaving to his Bulwark; awe is recoil from Him. "Together they constitute the foundation of halakhic religious consciousness" (70). In our blessings we begin by referring to God in the second person and end by referring to Him in the third person. The former expresses the sense of God's presence, the latter (the third-person reference) reflects our sense of God's concealment. In our *Kedushah* prayer, we declare both that His presence fills the earth and that His servants ask, "Where is the place of His honor?" Even though God is present everywhere, everyone asks where He is, for He dwells in seclusion.

IMITATIO DEI

Rabbi Soloveitchik identifies man's relating to God through a combination of love and awe with the principle of *imitatio Dei* – the imitation of God, as prescribed by the verse (in its rabbinic interpretation), "And you shall walk in His ways" (Deut. 28:9). He contrasts *imitatio* with *devekut*, cleaving to God (Deut. 11:22), first analyzing *imitatio Dei* as a kind of "second best" to cleaving, and then charting a course from imitation to *devekut*.

For Rabbi Soloveitchik, the key point about *imitatio Dei* is that it presents a solution to the contradiction between moral freedom and subjugation. The individual who strives to imitate God has despaired of cleaving to Him and has chosen a more realistic, attainable goal. Imitation, in other words, is a confession of failure to cleave. The individual who emulates God's deeds utilizes the revealed commands to express his freedom. It is as if the emulator were God's partner in legislating rules and commandments, even though those commands in truth are legislated from without.

But then – awe strikes. And then – joy is reawakened. And

then – once again the awareness of compulsion rises up. There is a dialectical movement of hope and disappointment, cleaving and departing, coming closer and becoming distant. *Imitatio Dei* reconciles the positions: Divine decree combines with individual freedom. Instead of feeling compelled to obey the Master for the sake of self-preservation, one willingly chooses to obey the Master out of recognition of His greatness. *Imitatio Dei* thus "has elements of both surrender and the exaltation of the free spirit" (77).

FROM *IMITATIO* TO *DEVEKUT*

Imitation is not enough; man must cleave to God. The Torah enjoins these as two separate *mitzvot*. But one is the route to the other. "Dialectical love – love that is cushioned with awe [as in *imitatio Dei*] – rises to the level of total, pure love [in cleaving]" (81). Cleaving, in other words, is absolute love, without the opposing movement of running away. It can be achieved not only in an eschatological future, but in the present.

The source of fear and fleeing from God "lies only in the surface layers of religious consciousness" (91). In the depths of that consciousness lies "an experience of seeking that is interwoven with the revelational vision" (ibid.). Thus "the man of God begins with duality" – the duality of love and terror – but "ends with unity" (ibid.), the unity of pure love. This experience reflects the idea that "the desire behind the revelation is not that the human being be subservient or fearful, but rather that he be totally redeemed" (92).

What, then, is the state of *devekut*? How is it attained? Rabbi Soloveitchik insists that cleaving should not be confused with the *unio mystica*, mystic unification. In the unification state, man has denied his essence, emptied out the content of his life to focus on an eternal point. Cleaving is different. The individual lives his own life, filled with goals and activities. Human uniqueness and originality are preserved.

The mystics failed to see the ethical nature of religion; outward behavior and action made no difference to them, for they believed that only ecstatic experiences count. They secluded themselves, abandoning social life. Negating society in this way entails negating the historical process in which the human spirit develops culture and forges society.

In stark contrast, the Sages interpreted "cleaving to Him" as cleaving to others, specifically to scholars, those who know God. "God joins with the individual only in the merit of the community which is loyal to Him and seeks Him" (89). An individual who secludes himself from the community cannot cleave to God. God's holiness will not be found unless ten are present. The individual fulfills his own essence through activities directed at both self and other, and he must link himself to the chain of historical events that form society.

WHAT IS CLEAVING?

As we saw, Judaism teaches that one cleaves to God by cleaving to those who know Him. But how do those individuals cleave to Him? The Rav's answer is: by their knowledge. Not abstract knowledge, however; rather, knowledge translated into will which then translates into action. God's pronouncement to Jeremiah captured this thought: "But let him that glories, glory in this, that he understands and knows Me, that I am the Lord who exercises lovingkindness, justice, and righteousness on the earth" (Jer. 9:23). The goal of knowledge is moral action, and thus, "Study and practice, knowledge and will, are blended together in a unified spiritual entity" (93).

How, though, does the achievement of the knowledge-will-action complex realize the ideal of cleaving? By way of reply the Rav refers to a principle articulated by, among others, Maimonides: in the act of knowing, the knower becomes one with the known. This principle applies both to God's knowledge and to the human being's knowledge.

In many instances of human knowledge – for example, "I know that the table is solid" – there is a differentiation between the knower, the subject, and the known, the object. Even in a statement like "I know that I exist," I split my personality, as it were, between the knowing subject and the known object. For God, however, as explained by Maimonides in the *Mishneh Torah*, there is a perfect unity – the knower is one with the known and with the knowledge. Further, God's knowledge of the world is one with knowledge of Himself, for the world cannot exist separately from God. The world is not an independent object.

The thesis that the knower is one with what is known is expounded by Maimonides in his *Mishneh Torah* with reference to God, and in his *Guide of the Perplexed* with reference to man. There is, to be sure, a certain type of knowledge in which one merely "photographs" what is known, with no active, creative input. But in other cases, the sort the Rav is interested in, cases of active, creative knowledge, the knower unites with the known. "When one grasps the intelligible essence of an entity, one penetrates it and unites with it…[one] takes it captive, and conjoins with it" (97). Despite the parallel between divine knowledge and human knowledge, a difference must be noted. Divine cognition has no end, since if God were to stop thinking about the world, all would revert to chaos; but human beings do not cognize continuously. At times, they know only potentially, and the dualism of subject and object is reinstated. Still, when man knows, his cognition blends and unites with the universe; He "conquers" it and conjoins with it.

The critical point now is this: when the individual unites with the world, he also unites with his Creator. For the world, the creation of God's thought, is the object of both God's knowledge and human knowledge. "By knowing the world the individual knows His Creator and cleaves to Him" (102), for "man and God are united in knowledge of the world" (103). God is united with the world, man is united with the world, and man is thus united with God.

But cleaving demands more than knowing; it entails knowledge, like God's, that unites thought, will and action. In Judaism, unlike Aristotle's ideal of the intellectual life, "knowledge without action serves no purpose" (104). Knowledge of the world as knowledge of the truth of the existence of God is also knowledge of His active will – the moral impulse.

In the Jewish liturgy, we do not pray, as mystics would, for the annihilation of the world, but for it to be repaired, for creatures to broaden their knowledge and deepen their understanding. This vision of knowledge shaping the entire universe can be fulfilled only when cognition is fraught with will and action. Such a vision is attained when the individual identifies with the revelational will as expressed in Halakhah, Jewish law. Halakhah emanates from God's thought/will. "[W]hen the halakhist adopts the thought of the Holy One, Blessed Be He, he identifies with the intellect and the primordial will of the One and unites with Him" (105).

The Rav concludes this part of his discussion by noting that our Sages identified two aspects of the fulfillment of the commandment to love God: 1) contemplating the acts of creation; 2) contemplating the word of God, the Halakhah. These two activities are precisely what is required for cleaving to God.

ELEVATING HUMAN CONSCIOUSNESS

According to the Rav, there are three ways in which Judaism expresses its desire to raise human consciousness to a spiritual one, thus linking the natural search for God to revelatory faith. These ways are (1) the rule of the intellect, (2) the elevation of the body, and (3) the perpetuity of God's word.

(1) "The rule of the intellect" refers to the fact that intellect is the final arbiter of Halakhah. The halakhist's exercise of intellect involves the construction of *hiddushim*, novel concepts, interpretations and ideas. These novellae must arise from within the bounds of certain fixed, *a priori* postulates given by revelation;

but the freedom of creative interpretation and conceptualization granted to halakhic personalities within these limits gives the lie to the allegation that Halakhah is ossified. *Rishonim* and *aharonim*, medieval and modern commentators, "created new worlds that are breathtaking in their beauty and sublimity" (108). In fact, the use of reason in halakhic thought not only creates new ideas, but infuses the fixed axioms of Halakhah with life and freshness. While the axioms are revealed and cannot be rejected, there is a "marvelous freedom" in the creative conceptual activity of the halakhist (109).

(2) We turn next to the elevation of the body, which the Rav regards as the basic teaching of the entire Torah. Judaism does not despair of the natural, biological aspect of the human being. It declares that the body's instinctual biological drives must be refined, redeemed and sanctified, instead of being extirpated. Through the imposition of *mitzvot* making demands of the body, those drives are stamped with "direction and purposefulness" (111). The Torah does not forbid man to indulge in pleasure, even though it forcefully prevents the body from being enslaved to pleasure and desire and from indulging in pleasure to excess.

For example, eating is bestial activity, yet the Torah commands the Jew, "You shall eat in the presence of the Lord your God" (Deut. 14:23). Notice: the prescription is to eat, not to pray! Even the most basic biological function can be harnessed to the service of God, and indeed become a source of sanctity. Jews are commanded to eat portions of sacrificed animals, second tithes (*ma'aser sheni*), matzah, etc. And they are to do in the manner of ordinary eating, while hungry, and not merely as a formal ritual act. These prescribed eatings give rise to emotions of awe and joy. In a similar fashion, ordinary, everyday meals must be devoted to discussions of Torah. Again, when people eat sacrificial meat and festive meals, they are also to feed strangers, orphans, and widows. Eating, then, according to Judaism, is both an act of religious worship, and one of social morality and connectedness. And so: "If man eats properly, in accordance with the requirements of the

Halakhah, then he is eating before God, serving Him with this 'despised' function, and cleaving to Him" (114).

Another illustration of the elevation of the body involves sexual intercourse. In contrast to Christianity and other philosophies, Judaism took a positive view of sexuality and marriage: "Be fruitful and multiply" (Gen. 1:28) is a command of the Torah; the Sages lauded the institution of marriage in high terms; a husband must have intercourse with his wife periodically and out of love and affection. Worship of the creator through one's body, the Rav states, "is preferable to worship through prayer" (115). As with eating, the key point is not to eradicate the body or escape from it, but to sanctify it through discipline. "By sanctifying the body [the Halakhah] creates one whole unit of psychosomatic man who worships God with his spirit and his body and elevates the beast [in him] to the eternal Heavens" (117).

The content of revelation is directed at a full natural existence; revelatory faith does not deny the significance of reality, but instead affirms it and links it to the attainment of transcendent values. And not only does the Halakhah adopt a realistic view of the human being in legislating concerning eating and sex, but we can state sweepingly that halakhic norms can be applied only via clear knowledge of the world. The Halakhah "is enclosed within the realm of the actual. Its object is the world that encompasses us completely" (120). Halakhah takes account of all scientific and technological innovations, and its articulation and application depends upon concepts like space, causation, intention, and compulsion, and on disciplines such as physiology, anatomy, astronomy and politics. Adapting Galileo's maxim that the book of Nature is written in the language of mathematics, Rabbi Soloveitchik states: "Halakhah writes in the language of orderly scientific reality" (121).

(3) "Perpetuity of God's word" refers to prophecy as well as (so we shall see later) to the ongoing process of the transmission of the Torah, the *masorah*. Prophecy reflects the same blending of revelation and reality that we have just seen. At the onset of

prophecy, God reveals Himself to man, transporting the prophet into a supra-rational world. But the prophet is commanded "to return to the actual world, to repair it and purify it" (123).

Even though God reveals Himself to human beings, He expects the individual to seek Him and to prepare for the prophetic encounter. The aspiring prophet must focus "on penetrating the secrets of the world, living a pure and holy life, perfecting one's halakhic ethical personality, and rising to the peak of cleaving to God" (123 24). He must purify and sanctify Himself, fulfilling the commandment, "You shall be holy" (Lev. 19:2).

The Rav allows that sometimes the revelation of the *Shekhinah* precedes human preparation and self-perfection. And in these instances, the natural consciousness and revelational consciousness are discontinuous with each other. But when the individual encounters God after seeking Him, then "the free creative consciousness unites with the 'compelled' revelational consciousness, and a relationship of question and answer, of longing and fulfillment, bursts forth" (126). This is not to say, however, that the revelation is brought about entirely by human effort. On the contrary, revelation of the *Shekhinah* occurs in a realm that is closed to the intellect.

The religious individual may well see disunity between the works of Creation ("the Hidden Intellect") and the Supernal Will of Mount Sinai. How does a revelational command afford an understanding of the real world? However, as one's knowledge deepens, one begins to apprehend the unity of Creation and Sinai. Rationality and revelation become one. The only difference is that Creation is a question, a mystery, while Sinai heralds the solution. "The weight of the irrationality and inconsistency in the perceived world lies heavily" upon cultural man, before he encounters revelation and grasps its depths (127). He finds his existential anchor and, even more significantly, affirmation of his personal uniqueness and independence precisely within the contents of revelation. The compulsion felt by man, binding him to the authority of the revelation, becomes his "savior." Revelation "frees him from the chains of the natural world and raises him to the level of freedom of the man of God" (128).

Thus, the individual begins with a search for freedom, encounters compulsion, but ends with the experience of freedom. "There is no one as free as one who is engaged in the study of Torah" (*Avot* 6:2). The experience of the commandments is one of joy, happiness, and total freedom, as if the divine commandments were identical with the demands of the creative rational mind. He fulfills the commandments not out of compulsion, nor out of emulation, but out of identification and partnership. Therefore, unlike the gentile sages, "the great Jewish sages were not tormented by the war against their instinctual drives" (129).

NATURE AND MORALITY

The Rav next elaborates upon the idea that Creation and Sinai are integrated. He asserts, in particular, that Creation attains its perfection in the revelation at Sinai.

In explaining this assertion, the Rav begins with the observation that the fact of existence results from a moral act – God's creation of a world that is "very good" (Gen. 1:31) is itself the supreme moral performance. Sinai is connected to Creation because, corresponding to the just-noted moral aspect of Creation, Sinai requires of man that he act morally. Indeed, the person bound by Sinai must imitate God's creating the world by himself repairing the world. By thus contributing to perfecting Creation, man rises to the highest moral level – "moral action is action interwoven with the drama of the great Creation" (134). The supreme human purpose is to live "a complete, perfected experience," while also taking part in elevating the existence of the other (131). (To put it another way: the ontological law of Creation is revealed to human beings in the form of the revelational command of Sinai.) The imperative to seek moral perfection entails endorsement of a vision that is permeated with optimism.

Because it stresses repairing and completing this world, Judaism thirsts for the concrete life and "hates death" (132). In Jewish law, dead bodies must be separated from the sacral; and the commandment to save life is heavily emphasized. The emphasis on concrete existence underscores the fact, discussed earlier, that Judaism does not "separate the eternal from the temporal" (ibid.). In other words: it does not ignore this world. "The Kingdom of Heaven is like the Kingdom of Earth" (*Berakhot* 58a). Practice of Halakhah sanctifies the profane, elevating the world and crowning it with a renewed soul. The world "acquires eternal holiness, and unites with its Creator" (133).

Judaism's this-worldly emphasis is also manifest in its teaching that miracles occur only when absolutely necessary, when all other means have been exhausted. Judaism extols lawfulness and the natural order; orderly creation, not miraculous intervention, reveals the glory of God.

JOINING THE PROPHETIC TRADITION

It is not only prophets who achieve the fulfillment of the hope to cleave to the Divinity. Rather, "all Jews can fulfill their aspiration toward God by joining the prophetic tradition" (134). For God's revelation is "an eternal vision that sails in the stream of time and the flow of the generations" (135). The eternal enters the flow of temporal experience.

The Rav argues that revelation never ends, using the following line of thought. God relates to man both as an inseparable part of the world, and in and of himself. The Creator reveals Himself with the name "Elokim," as the possessor of power relating to the natural world. But He reveals Himself to spiritual man with His special, "personal" name, the Tetragrammaton. "When the infinite 'I' connects with man, man is redeemed from a closed-off natural existence and is raised to a unique personal level of existence" (136). The revelation lifts a person from object to subject, from the level of "living thing" to "person." It is for this reason that the revelation never ends, because if it did, "the unique personal consciousness of the real world would come to an end." According to the Midrash, the souls of all of the Jewish people throughout history stood at Sinai – a teaching that brings to the fore the possibility of all Jews participating in prophecy.

TRANSMITTING THE MASORAH

The proposition that the revelation does not end is reflected in the transmission and reception of the Torah, which joins together generations and eras. Reading the Torah aloud in the synagogue is meant to revive the experience of standing at Mount Sinai. Hence the view of Rabbi Meir of Rothenburg that one must stand during the synagogue reading of the Torah. Hence also the practice of reading the Ten Commandments in public using a special grouping of the verses into one verse, because this imitates God's utterance of the commandments. (By contrast, when one studies the Torah, each verse is read as a separate unit.)

When a teacher transmits his teaching, he is not only transmitting information. He is uniting with the disciple, and likewise when prophets communicate to people, they bestow their personal glory and share some of their essence. (This point is manifest in Moses sharing some of his glory with his disciple Joshua [Num. 27:20] and with the seventy elders [Num. 11:17].) If a student grasps what the teacher does, they have joined, by virtue of principle that knower and known are one. This is especially true of the study of the Oral Torah, "a Torah which by its nature and application can never be objectified, even after it has been written down. 'Oral Torah' means a Torah that blends with the individual's personal uniqueness and becomes an inseparable part of man. When the person then transmits it to someone else, his personal essence is transmitted along with it" (142). According to the Sages, disciples are called children because "the essence of their spiritual personality emanates, and is born, from the bosom of the teacher" (ibid.).

Rabbi Soloveitchik vividly and charmingly illustrates the nature of *masorah* by recounting a childhood experience. While yet a boy, he would listen from his room to his father studying Torah with a small group of Torah scholars. His father would present a difficulty in a ruling of the Rambam (for example, one posed by his arch-critic Rabad). Various answers would be proposed by the participants; his father would find them unsatisfactory. Then, however, his father would find a way to defend the Rambam. The Rav says that he felt that "the Rambam himself was present in the room, listening to what my father was saying…sitting with me on my bed" (144). He would jump out bed, run to his mother, and proclaim to her excitedly, "The Rambam is right, he defeated the Rabad. Father came to his aid." At times, however, his father would not find a solution. But his mother reassured him that his father would find one – and even if not, perhaps he himself will when he grows up. "The main thing," she told him, "is to learn Torah with joy and excitement" (145).

Reflecting on this childhood experience, the Rav writes of its impact in later years:

> When I sit down to study the Torah, I find myself immediately in the company of the sages of the *masorah*. The relations between us are personal. The Rambam is at my right, Rabbenu Tam at my left, Rashi sits up front and interprets, Rabbenu Tam disputes him; the Rambam issues a ruling, and the Rabad objects. They are all in my little room, sitting around my table… [Studying Torah] is a powerful experience of becoming friends with many generations of Torah scholars, the joining of one spirit with another, the union of souls. Those who transmitted the Torah and those who received it come together in one historical way-station (145).

Teaching and transmitting Torah is an act of *hesed*, loving-kindness. Prophets and wise men are "guardians for the distribution of spiritual wealth" (146). Prophecy involves "existential coupling" with the community as the prophet shares the revelation (147).

It is by "an act of historical identification with the past and future, the fate and destiny, of the Jewish people" (ibid.) that individual and community come together. *Keneset Yisrael*, the community of Israel, refers to "the coupling of the first and last generations of prophet and listener" (ibid.).

RABBI SOLOVEITCHIK'S SUMMATION

In the short concluding section of the essay, the Rav summarizes the three stages of religious development that he has outlined. A state of trust alternating with fear evolves into a state of love combined with awe, and from there to a state of love characterized by desire and cleaving. Man begins his quest in a state of freedom, "striving for the absolute, for the noncontingent and the eternal." Yet reason alone cannot grasp these, and he is confronted with a coercive revelation that seems to deny his freedom and his values. Man tries to link his revelational experience of God with his experience of God within a lawful, orderly nature, and comes to "befriend the revelational experience" (149). Fear turns into awe and is accompanied by joy in performing the commandments, as man tries to emulate God. Revelation is no longer seen as alien and threatening; though it is imposed upon him, it grants him support and tranquility. At the highest stage, the revelatory command is no longer external to him at all. Revelation, far from being a threat to his freedom, is now its very source and affirmation. Man has entered into partnership with God and attained "the wonder of the identification of wills" (150).

The preceding summary describes only the text section of *And From There You Shall Seek*. The notes add a great deal of significant material, and many of them are mini-essays in their own right. The topics covered include the interpretation of the Song of Songs, divine love, the relationship between philosophical proofs of God and religious experience, revelation and reason, Kabbalistic motifs, the structure of blessings, the names of God, the sanctification of the land, and festival rejoicing.

CLOSING REMARKS:
U-VIKKASHTEM MI-SHAM AND *ISH HA-HALAKHAH*

Now that we have considered some of the major themes of *And From There You Shall Seek*, a few very brief comments are in order regarding its place in Rabbi Soloveitchik's oeuvre.

'The Rav, as we said, drafted *U-Vikkashtem mi-Sham* in the mid-1940's. This was a period of immense creativity during which he wrote three major works – *Ish ha-Halakhah*, *The Halakhic Mind* (written in 1944, published in 1986), and *Ish ha-Elokim*, the ancestor of *U-Vikkashtem mi-Sham*. It is difficult to know why he published *Ish ha-Halakhah* soon after its composition but waited so long before publishing the other two. Perhaps he felt impelled to publish *Ish ha-Halakhah* because it contained an element of eulogy for his father, Rabbi Moshe Soloveitchik, who had died in 1941. But the postponement of the other works is curious, and Rabbi Soloveitchik left no indication of its cause. What can be noted, though, is that when *The Halakhic Mind* finally appeared, it was in its 1944 incarnation, without any changes except the title and the omission of several technical footnotes. In contrast, *U-Vikkashtem mi-Sham* (then *Ish ha-Elokim*) underwent rewriting prior to its publication – rewriting that apparently involved more than merely reorganizing or putting fine touches on sentences. The first revision we know of was done during the 1960's, when the Rav prepared the essay for publication in *Talpiyot*, the journal that had published *Ish ha-Halakhah* two decades earlier. This revised manuscript was lost, but a photocopy of the original, un-revised manuscript eventually was located, and Rabbi Solovcitchik once again revised and expanded the essay in the 1970's. The work we have certainly differs from the original essay of the 1940's.

There can be little doubt that the three works from the

1940's – *Ish ha-Halakhah*, *The Halakhic Mind*, and *Ish ha-Elokim* – are parts of an ambitious intellectual program and are related to one another in various ways, involving both comparisons and contrasts. In the aforementioned 1963 letter to Dr. Mirsky, Rabbi Soloveitchik characterizes the unpublished essay that was to become *U-Vikkashtem mi-Sham* as "a continuation of my first essay on the halakhic man." The aim of the unpublished essay, he continues, is "to trace out the portrait of the character of the halakhic man in terms of his inner world, his experience and his desire to run toward the Holy One, Blessed Be He." The Rav's declaration to Dr. Mirsky that the essay he had "hidden away" was a continuation of *Ish ha-Halakhah* suggests a particular relationship between the two works: to wit, that *U-Vikkashtem mi-Sham* fills out the portrait of halakhic man by exploring his inner world and religious experience, perhaps even exposing facets of his personality and development omitted in the earlier essay. Of interest also is that the Rav himself proposed the title of the book that contains both *Ish ha-Halakhah* and *U-Vikkashtem mi-Sham*, namely *Ish ha-Halakhah: Galuy Ve-Nistar* (*Halakhic Man: Revealed and Hidden* [Jerusalem, 1979]). The implication of the subtitle is that *Ish ha-Halakhah* portrays the "external" aspect of halakhic man, while *U-Vikkashtem mi-Sham* captures the hidden, inner core. On such a reading, the "cleaving" personality depicted as the apex of the three-stage process in *U-Vikkashtem mi-Sham* presumably would be identical to halakhic man. Since *U-Vikkashtem mi-Sham* focuses more on the development of "cleaving man" rather than simply on his phenomenology, another way of stating the relationship between the two works would be that whereas *Ish ha-Halakhah* presents halakhic man analytically – breaking down the whole into parts – *U-Vikkashtem mi-Sham* is synthetic, showing how a halakhic personality may be built.[8]

Yet while there are clearly points of contact between halakhic man and the "cleaving" personality described in the final section of *U-Vikkashtem mi-Sham* – most prominently, halakhic creativity and the "identity of wills" – the two typological individuals appear to differ in several ways. For example, "cleaving man" is open to mystical themes, while halakhic man is not. Also, when confronted by reality, halakhic man, like the scientist, tends to quantify and classify, while "cleaving man" is attracted as well by those qualitative aspects of reality that cannot be quantified. Moreover, the process of development undergone by "cleaving man," which involves broad cultural engagement and a diverse range of experiences, does not sit easily with the more narrowly focused outlook and austere nature of halakhic man. In both his personality and his religious approach, "cleaving man" displays a multidimensionality that, *prima facie*, is lacking in halakhic man.

A case can be made that these divergences are only apparent. But if one chooses to acknowledge them, several explanations of the differences present themselves. It is conceivable that, whatever the author's intentions, halakhic man and cleaving man present two different models of Jewish religiosity; it is also possible that cleaving man encompasses halakhic man and goes beyond him; or perhaps Rabbi Soloveitchik's view of halakhic man evolved between the publication of the two works. This much we can say with confidence: regardless of whether one should read *Ish ha-Halakhah* and *U-Vikkashtem mi-Sham* in conjunction to understand the respective works, one must certainly read them in conjunction in order to understand their author. It is precisely the breadth, depth, and originality of his vision that make these works so compelling – and assure them a permanent place in the canon of Jewish and general religious thought.

*　*　*

Creating this volume was a complex task. We and the essay's translator were fortunate to be assisted by talented and erudite collaborators.

With great devotion to the project, Mark Steiner carefully reviewed the draft manuscript and refined it with consummate skill. At a later stage, Atara Segal likewise examined the entire essay closely and consistently contributed excellent suggestions and refinements. Rabbi Aharon Lichtenstein meticulously and patiently answered queries, resolved quandaries, and provided formulations for a variety of difficult passages. Rabbi Mosheh Lichtenstein carefully sorted through nuances and suggested valuable revisions.

In addition, we thank Robert Milch and Shifra Schapiro for copy editing; Meira Mintz for compiling the subject index; Marc Herman for compiling the source index; the latter two, along with Aharon Bejell, Doron Friedlander, Nadine Gesundheit, and David Shabtai, for help with proofreading and source checking; Yosef Avivi for assistance in locating passages in Kabbalistic literature; and David Berger, Mordechai Cohen, Daniel Frank, and Warren Zev Harvey for advising on the translation or formulation of certain passages.

Finally, Bernard Scharfstein and Adam Bengal of Ktav, along with others involved in the technical aspects of producing the book, evinced their dedication to the Rav and his writings by their consistently gracious accommodation and cooperation.

We are grateful to all.

NOTES

1. Published in 1944 in the rabbinic journal *Talpiyot*, and translated into English by Lawrence Kaplan as *Halakhic Man* (Philadelphia, 1983).
2. Rabbi Joseph B. Soloveitchik, *Community, Covenant and Commitment: Selected Letters and Communications*, ed. Nathaniel Helfgot (Jersey City, 2005), 321–22.
3. *Community, Covenant and Commitment*, 322.
4. Although for most of the work the search is that of the individual rather than (as in Deuteronomy) the search of the Jewish people, the communal theme emerges by the essay's end.
5. The title of the section – "Overt Halakhah and Concealed Love," which, as noted earlier, Rabbi Soloveitchik used as the book's title in the letter to Dr. Mirsky – conveys an important theme of the essay. Halakhah is not simply about the overt, the external; a proper orientation to Halakhah will contain certain emotions as well, including love.

This does not mean only that mitzvah observance contains an emotional component. For it is also the case that Halakhah expresses love on the part of both God (who gave it) and man (who performs it).

6. This criticism is based on objections that were *de rigueur* at the time *U-Vikkashtem mi-Sham* was drafted. Today, proofs for God's existence are again in vogue, even though atheism remains strong.

7. Note that "creation" is generally a translation for *Bereshit*, not *yetzirah*; i.e., it refers to that which has been created, not to the act of creating.

8. See Aviezer Ravitzky, "Rabbi J.B. Soloveitchik on Human Knowledge: Between Maimonidean and Neo-Kantian Philosophy," *Modern Judaism* 6:2 (1986): 157–88.

"Like a hind yearning for water brooks,
my soul yearns for You, O God"
(Ps. 42:2)

In memory of my wife Tonya ז״ל,
a woman of refinement

ᔐ Chapter One
Overt Halakhah and Covert Love

A

*A*s the setting sun of the Sabbath eve ignites the western horizon, and the Sabbath Queen, delicate, pleasing, and graceful as a bride, emerges from the rosy blaze of sunset, the strains of the Song of Songs course into a world becoming pure and sanctified, wrapped in the serenity of calmness and rest.

The Shulammite, blackened by the sun, yearns for her heart's chosen one. Her lover, who pastures his flock among the lilies, has sworn eternal love to his pure dove. The lover longs for his faithful bride; his soul thirsts for her.

The most beautiful of women wanders about within the city walls in the pale, moon-enchanted nights. Early in the dewy, sun-drenched mornings she goes out into the orchards. She is looking for the beloved of her soul, who is standing among the shadows, watching from the byways, peering through the cracks. Lovesick, she searches for her partner. She searches for him but cannot find him. Has her lover left her and forgotten her for eternity? Has he forgotten the affection of their wedding day and departed from her forever?

The lad with the beautiful eyes skips along the hills, toward his dear bride. He pursues the Shulammite, who hides in rock crannies and behind cliffs. He is attracted by her grace, her image continually before his eyes. He is full of longing, aflame with yearning. With quick steps he approaches his partner, but he does not meet her. The hour of their meeting has arrived; at this very moment the lad retreats and hides among the rocks.

"You are beautiful, my beloved, your eyes are doves," he sings (Song of Songs 1:15), hidden among the ancient, glorious hills. He sees her, but cannot be seen. He is very, very close to her, but also immeasurably distant.

"And you, my beloved, are handsome and pleasing," she replies (Song 1:16) from among the tender river-shoots. Trembling, she rushes out to greet her lover. Her heart pounds: Will he appear from the quiet, glowing horizon? Will he alight before her in the orchard lanes? She hears the rustle of footsteps on the hills, in the valleys, among the tender river-shoots, and in the garden paths where the almond and pomegranate trees blossom. She bestirs herself and goes out to greet him.

Suddenly the echo melts away and disappears in the sun-drenched distance. He will love her forever; he will always remember the grace of her youth. Just as the bridegroom delights in his bride, so will he delight in her. He has not sent his partner away, nor has he handed her a bill of divorce. Yet, in spite of all this, their love cannot be realized, their yearning cannot be fulfilled completely. But why? Why must he flee from her at the moment that she pursues him? Why does he not look and see that she is mad with longing and yearning? Why does he not say to her, "Lift your eyes and see that I have fulfilled my vow and arrived"?

B

The beloved returns home from her wanderings from mountain to mountain, from hill to hill, along winding roads and twisting paths. Tensely alert, her entire being pleads for her lover's arrival. She is a tempest of yearning for him, totally absorbed in listening for the slightest rustle. Her whole being asks, "Where has my beloved gone?" Her entire self pleads, "If you meet my beloved, tell him this: that I am faint with love" (Song 5:8). She sobs in her agony, loneliness, and suffering.

Suddenly her lover appears from the obscurity of the dark night, knocking on his dear one's door and whispering faithfully, "Let me in, my sister, my darling, my faultless dove! For my head is drenched with dew, my locks with the drops of the night" (Song 5:2). Now I have arrived, I have kept my word, I have fulfilled the vision. Your desire has been fulfilled, your longing has not been in vain. I have yearned for you; I, the companion of your youth, am now here. You shall follow me and never be separated from me.

The beloved awakens from her sleep and listens to the gentle voice of her lover. His voice burns its way into her heart, kindling there an ancient flame. It is suffused with both enchantment and desire.

Nevertheless, the beloved refuses to rise from her bed and open the door to her lover. The cold of the moonless, starless night, deep weariness, laziness, and fear combine to paralyze her will and bind her legs. Why should she refuse to undo the latch and open the door to her lover? Hasn't she been searching for him day and night? Hasn't she been pursuing him, asking passersby if they have seen him, adjuring the daughters of Jerusalem (Song 2:7, 3:5) and suffering insults, blows, and spiritual torment on his behalf? What has happened? Has all her sense of yearning evaporated under the oppressive torpor of loneliness just at the moment when her lover has arrived? Has the hidden force that stirred her spirit during the days filled with wandering and the nights filled with anticipation and anxiety subsided just at the moment that her lover has fulfilled his pledge and his footsteps are heard at the entrance to her tent? Does desire no longer permeate her being, is the urgency no longer alive within her? At the very moment of fulfillment and realization, the hour of redemption and deliverance, has it all vanished and been silenced? "I have taken off my robe – am I to don it again? I have bathed my feet – am I to soil them again?" she responds in lunatic indifference (Song 5:3).

Yet, after a moment the beloved leaps off her bed, her hands dripping myrrh on the handles of the bolt. She opens her abode to her lover. The flame of yearning is sparked once again; her spirit is restored. Her love rages. Her soul's joy returns. Her heart is afraid yet expands toward her lover. The door opens – but the lover is not there. "I rose to let in my beloved.... But my beloved had turned and gone!" (Song 5:5–6).

C

The scarlet-clad daughters of Jerusalem are astonished, and they whisper among themselves. This sort of game – what is its character? The guards on the city walls doze off in the dimness of the cold night and sink into a wondrous dream about the desired one, overflowing with love, who has promised his beloved eternal affection yet runs away from her, and about the daughter of nobles, drunk with yearning, who seeks her soulmate yet eludes him. A lover who yearns yet hides, a bride who conceals herself – what does this mean? As the last rays of the sun set and the dimness of the twilight between the profane weekday and the sacred Sabbath approaches, both the reader of the Song of Songs and the listener are confused, asking, "This mischievous game of enamoredness and rejection, of running after and running away, of tension and disappointment, of searching and hiding, of disclosure and concealment – what does it mean?"

Steeping themselves in this paradoxical love and this strange yet bold and adventurous yearning, those who observe the Sabbath and call it a delight invite the lover to go out and greet his bride, the Sabbath Queen, and invite the beloved to answer her lover's knock, to be her husband's crowning glory and to bring him into her dwelling safely and joyously. But will they meet?

D

The Halakhah asserts, "All the Scriptures are holy, but the Song of Songs is the holy of holies" (*Mishnah Yadayim* 3:5).[1] The Song of Songs is the most wonderful and most astonishing poem of the divine ontic dialectics. It is the poem of the creation and the Creator in general, and of the Jewish nation and its God in particular.

The sun-blackened Shulammite – the creation – in her lowly, turbid state yearns for her heart's choice: God.

The lover/Creator loves His beloved/creation.

The Creator has captured the heart of His creation; the Eternal has captivated the spirit of every living thing.

The Creator has promised the creation that He will never abandon her. The creation has drawn the Creator's heart with one of her eyes that gaze upon the face of eternity. Finitude has drawn the heart of infinitude with one coil of her necklace.

The Creator loves His creation, yet He nevertheless rests in a hidden place, in the shade.

The creation craves her Creator, yet she nevertheless refuses to open the doors of her dwelling![2]

≥ Chapter Two

The Yearning Heart

"Draw me after you, let us run!" (Song 1:4).

A

*H*ow does the creation search for its Creator? There are four realms in which man seeks the image of the Creator as reflected in creation, [which includes] being, nature, and spirit: (1) the cosmic drama; (2) the depths of his spiritual existence; (3) the system of *a priori* concepts; (4) a particular religious facticity and transcendental "experience." In these areas, religious reason explores the following elements respectively: (a) the lawfulness of the effect (the first cause, the telos, and the continuity of the causal order as well as the ruptures within it); (b) the complex of moral will which is manifested, paradoxically, in the joint consciousness of absolute freedom and of total obligation; the call of conscience and the despondency of the sinning soul; the aesthetic experience intertwined with the vision of transfinite sublimity; the order of cultural values; the metaphysical yearning; the essence and process of cognition, and the like; (c) the pinnacle of the system of pure concepts of the understanding, the *a priori* concept of deity, distinct from any psychophysical experience, as the essential crowning jewel of being; (d) the sense of absolute dependence; the frustrated yearnings pulsating in man's spirit; the ecstasy of the mystical masters; the intuition of a supra-sensible realm, and the like.

There is no hidden corner of the natural or spiritual world which man's consciousness, pining for its divine beloved, does not peer into and scrutinize. Human consciousness carefully investigates the buds of transcendence that appear every so often in the spiritual desert. This search is not the romantic yearning of fugitives from the monotonous secularism of the everyday. Rather, it is rooted in the general cultural consciousness. Flesh-and-blood man longs to escape from the straits of the limited, bounded, and contingent world and go out into the limitless, independent, wide-open spaces. This search is an act of self-transcendence, which is truly the essence of man's cultural ascent.

The question of whether the Deity's connection with the world is transcendent or immanent is irrelevant. Man sometimes attempts to find God within reality, and sometimes beyond it. It all depends on the viewpoint of the inidividual who searches. There are many facets to man's awareness of God, which is replete with the absolute and the eternal, yet reverberates within a contingent, temporal creature. It listens for the occasional notes of the old-new song that bursts forth from without as well as from within reality, attesting to a wondrous supermundane being that, in the Kabbalists' phrase, "fills and surrounds all the worlds" (*Tanya* 1:3, 41, 46; *Nefesh ha-Hayyim* 3:4). The mystical masters justly taught that the Deity separates itself from the existent, which is imprinted with the stamp of creation and chained by the constraints of objective cosmic necessity, yet at the same time dwells within it as one "who dwells with them in their impurity" (Lev. 16:16). The *Shekhinah* imbues both object and subject, yet also transcends them. God created the world, and His primordial will exists within it. *Malkhut* (Kingship) is the name the Kabbalists gave to the *Shekhinah* hidden within the lawfulness of nature and spirit, but God dwells beyond the limits of reality in infinite eternity.

Seeking God through the external and the internal worlds is not a theological issue of interest only to scholars of religion. It is a fundamental problem that arose at the dawn of human culture. From the time of the Greek philosophers to that of the masters of modern philosophy (not to mention the sages of the theocentric Eastern cultures), the search for God has resounded throughout the intellectual world. It takes different forms in accordance with the historical and cultural peculiarities of each epoch; it conceals and disguises itself in the range of concepts and variegated aspects through which each generation expresses its thoughts and internal struggles, but it never disappears entirely from the horizon of inquiry.

Even mathematicians do not deny this fact. The divine mystery remains in place even in the field of scientific knowledge, whenever it transcends the limits of precise physical experimentation and enters the realm of philosophical or metaphysical thought. Science indeed admits that it cannot explain a spatiotemporal phenomenon by a transcendental idea, for it cannot transcend its own limits and escape the circle of categorial assumptions corresponding to critical scientific experience, which is limited to the domain of finite perception and thought. Science does, however, admit to the presence of an irrational element in any world-view, and does not deny the right of others to investigate it.

Were one to ask, "What is the irrationality hovering over the pure scientific conception?" the answer would be that it is the realm of the qualitative and sensory. Modern physics, which has given such great prominence to the symbolic character of scientific constructions, knows that it cannot provide satisfactory explanations for one who aspires to penetrate the innerness and essence of being. In the qualitative reality as we experience it, there is no relativity, there is no quantitative reciprocity, nor are there mathematical equations. The world – as perceived by sensuality involving the process of stimulus and feeling, which fills our consciousness, enchants us with its variety of tones and colors, encompasses us completely, oppresses us with all the burden of its otherness, and amazes us with its size and its force – remains unexplained by science. Aristotelian physics attempted to explain reality through its true essence and its experienced qualities. But it failed and misled people for many centuries, because it led them to believe sincerely in the possibility of intellectual enlightenment about qualitative being. Both classical and modern physics have abandoned this daring enterprise. The creators of modern science are aware of the irrational character of the world as it appears to us in its everyday primitive concreteness, and they have despaired of any scientific achievements in this respect. The deeper truth that has been revealed to them is that they must give up the vain attempts of the ancients to understand the essence of phenomena, and concentrate instead on creating abstract constructions composed of mathematical formulas corresponding to concrete objects.

[In modern science] the sensory content of colors, sounds, heat, and odors, to which regularity and lawfulness do not apply, have been turned into pure quantities. [Quantitative] correlatives of this sort, whose entire meaning is not intrinsic within themselves but lies only in their mutual relations, have become the objects of scientific inquiry. According to the modern scientific-philosophical view, experience and theoretical inquiry belong to different realms. Experience belongs to the realm of actual living concreteness, theoretical inquiry to the realm of formal abstraction. There is a correspondence, but one cannot speak of identity. The abstract objects resulting from cognition do not explain our flowing, transitory world. This experiential world is not subject to scientific explanation, which is devoted only to pure, immutable correlation. Cognitive-scientific man duplicates the cosmic process by creating a formal correlative of the original, rationally inaccessible phenomenon.

The philosophical background of this scientific endeavor is the "faith" in a "mysterious" correspondence and in a parallelism between the two realms: the formal, mathematical realm and the actual, qualitative one. And indeed, experience has not disappointed this scientific "faith." It seems as though a thread of rationality winds its way through the fabric of the inanimate world.

In spite of its non-rationality and its otherness, it can be grasped by autonomous creative reason as a structure with certain relations. This view, however, does not explain the qualitative occurrences. Scientific man is aware of the mutual interconnections of the correlatives, and he expects a correspondence between the structures of the mind and the sequence of concrete phenomena. But the mind, caught in a metaphysical storm, will not be satisfied by abstract constructions or the matching of sequences. Quantitative, mathematical explanations, although they have immense technological consequences, do not provide answers to the greatest of man's questions: What is the nature, the meaning, and the value of reality? From [Friedrich] Schelling and [Søren] Kierkegaard to [Henri] Bergson, [Edmund] Husserl, and the other masters of existentialist philosophy and modern metaphysics, human thought has continued to rebel against the scientific, symbolic, *a priori* approach and has refused to recognize it as a solution to its bewilderment. The neo-realistic schools, which attempted to defend the formal, quantitative descriptions and explanations of phenomena, do not assuage the mind of the person of profound thought who demands intimate acquaintance with reality. The cry bursting from the soul longing for infinity breaks through all contemporary philosophical thought, rebelling against the formal cognition of creative reason as a response to the soul's greatest question.

B

We do not deny that there is a certain difference between past and present ways of thinking about seeking the infinite through finite reality. Whereas medieval and early modern philosophy expressed the search for infinity and eternity in objective terms – by formulating ostensibly decisive, logically valid proofs – the contemporary conception dares to deny the logical, objective validity of these proofs, which were based on categorial assumptions, such as that of substance or causality.[3] The contemporary conception asserts that we have no right to use these categories, which result from our finite, contingent, temporal existence, to prove the truth of an infinite, absolute, eternal reality. These categories – beneficial when used to determine formal, quantitative laws and to create the structures of the scientific world – cannot transcend the system of scientific empiricism and take absolute control over a transsensual, transexperiential, transintelligible world.

However, while this conception was intended to uproot and deny, it found itself implanting and affirming. It denied the possibility of using logical proofs to make indirect inferences from finitude to infinity, from temporality to eternity, and from actuality to transcendence. But instead of abolishing all these proofs, it accepted them anew as immediate experiences that are not based on logical inferences, but rather are manifested in sudden revelations and insights. These experiences have nothing in common with indirect inference or logical deduction. Just as consciousness of the world in general, and of the self in particular, do not involve logical demonstrations but constitute the spiritual essence of man, so too with the experience of the divine. It is totally aboriginal, the beginning and end of man's reality. It is forever prior to inference or deduction. It is the most certain of all certainties, the truest of truths. If there is a world, if anything at all is real – and no one who has not been ensnared by vain sophistries has any doubt about this – then there is a God who is the foundation and origin of everything that exists. If there is a self, if man exists – and this, too, all human beings know with certainty – then there is a living personal God who fills the consciousness of the self. It is impossible to think, to speak, to discuss the reality of the world and the reality of man without living and sensing the source of being: "I am that I am" (Ex. 3:14).

The basic principle of all basic principles and the pillar of all sciences is to know that there is a First Existent who brought every existing thing into being. All existing things, whether celestial, terrestrial, or belonging to an intermediate class, exist only through His true existence. If it could be supposed that He did not exist, it would follow that nothing else could possibly exist. If, however, it were supposed that all other beings were non-existent, He alone would still exist. Their nonexistence would not involve His nonexistence (Maimonides, *Mishneh Torah*, Laws of the Foundations of the Torah 1:1–3).[4]

The religious sensibility does not offer decisive proofs, draw inferences, or make deductions. It "senses" and experiences God in its innermost ontological consciousness. Without Him, there is no reality. "Taste and see how good is the Lord; happy is the man who takes refuge in Him!" (Ps. 34:9). Just as someone who sees a tree does not deduce indirectly that there are roots under the ground – for in the very perception of the trunk there is knowledge of the roots – so too man has no need to draw conclusions about God, for he knows God directly through the world. The words of Isaiah (40:26), "Lift high your eyes and see: Who created these?" or the rabbinic statement that there cannot be an illuminated castle without an owner or leader (*Gen. Rabbah* 39:1) are not meant to refer to abstract logical proofs or complicated demonstrations. On the contrary, they refer to the immediate awareness that overcomes man who sees God in the innermost essence of the world as well as in its surroundings.

Moreover, these immediate experiences are dynamic approaches, or, more accurately, powerful aspirations. In place of the contemplative medieval demonstrations, which lack vitality and force, there have appeared strong, powerful spiritual and emotional movements that draw their strength from their awareness of the mystery and inconclusiveness of being. The problematic of reality hints at and winks toward the secret of creation, and whispers that secret within man. This secret cannot be captured by symbolic, scientific solutions and cannot be illuminated by the radiance of the creative mind.[5] Only outside of formal symbolic cognition, with its free structures of thought, can the secret be revealed. Man's transcendental consciousness does not need any categorial mechanism. It can therefore reveal even what the *logos* cannot. [Immanuel] Kant's teaching, despite all the difficulties it has encountered, has not been undermined. Reason does not photograph the "given" but adapts it to its own needs. It sculpts the "given" with the chisel of categorial concepts so as to prepare it for scientific understanding. If reason is not accepting or passive; if, on the contrary, it is active, creative, and original; if its achievement is not, as realists have believed since the time of Aristotle, to describe the "given" as it is, but to create constructions and ideal symbols – and the fathers of modern physics agree with Kant that this is the case – then, as mentioned above, reason cannot govern an absolute, non-contingent realm, a realm which cannot be symbolized by the free creations of contingent understanding. The Deity is not subject to the intellect of His creatures, and the experience of God, infinity, and eternity is not confined to the particular extent of the finite, temporal mind.

Yet, what is impossible for the serene mind is well within the capacity of the storm-tossed experience and mighty aspiration that result from the direct confrontation between man and a world enveloped in the divine presence. If the experience of God in man's confrontation with reality is expressed not by demonstrations based on the complexities of the act of abstraction, but rather by a feeling of the sudden revelation of a direct, unmediated fact within our consciousness of being, then perception of the world itself becomes perception of God, and all the demonstrations resurface in a new form. A demonstration now means the experience of the creature yearning for the Creator. There are hints in the world that turn man's mind toward Heaven. Even Kant admitted this when he defined the three concepts – God, man, and the world – as regulative ideas. Even though the mind is unable to realize its absolute purpose, it establishes indicators that are directed toward its final end. "God, God," is written on the crossroads of existence. The human bond to God is expressed in aspiration, not in casuistry; in yearning, not in clever logical acrobatics.[6]

God is revealed to man through these very aspirations and yearnings. Why does man know no rest? Why does he seek that which he shall never find? It can only be that God draws man to Him. Man is tired and weary, dissatisfied with his life and his achievements; he is confused and lost in the paths of existence and cannot attain what he wants most. But the failure of his search does not prevent him from continuing to seek that which he cannot find. This "something" gives him no rest; it stimulates his nerves, attracting him with enormous power. What is the nature of the search? It is nothing but a search for God. What is the mysterious "something" that eludes man's grasp each time? It is total attachment to God, the Source of all sources. In man's yearning and frustration, God is revealed. The ontological consciousness, which is all yearning and upward striving, becomes identified with the transcendental consciousness. The world is nothing but the glory emanating from the Infinite. Eyes thirsty for the richness of being, and hungry for the abundance of the creation, see God; the soul, seized by vision and agitated by beauty, travels through existence, following the footsteps of the lover who is hiding in the crannies of the symbolic mind.[7]

c

From this viewpoint, man's ontological experience manifests itself in two aspects: (1) as scientific experience, which is relative, limited, and contingent, producing an ideal-functional correlative that corresponds to unexplained, alien being; (2) as transcendental experience – experience of the absolute infinite within the temporal, bounded and contingent; encounter with the Creator within the creation as its origin and end. The first type of experience is formulated in symbolic mathematical equations, and the second in continuous yearning and wondrous immediate experience, which burst forth from the depths of human experience and sweep the individual to mysterious faraway realms. There is religious facticity just as there is scientific facticity. There is religious reality, just as there is scientific reality. These refer to experiencing the world as aspiring toward God, as a living, bubbling, effervescent consciousness, burning with the flame of pent-up longing, which cannot be overcome by symbolic, relative logic. The scientific as well as the sensual, qualitative perception of the world, the consciousness of the self as well as the lofty aesthetic experience – all these can turn into a great, sublime, enduring transcendental experience: an experience of the Creator. It is related that, prior to his discovery of the ontological proof of God's existence, one of the great non-Jewish philosophers [Anselm of Canterbury] fasted for three consecutive days, praying and beseeching his Creator to enlighten him with a valid proof of His existence. Kierkegaard ridiculed him, saying, "You fool, does a baby in his father's arms need proofs or signs that the father exists? Does a person who feels the need to pray to God require a philosophical demonstration?" [Cf. the 1853 journal entry, "Curious Self-Contradiction."] In a whispered prayer to Him, man finds God.

As mentioned above, the consciousness of transcendent being is not a logical deduction but a wondrous striving upward with strength and courage, a conquest of the relative, contingent world by an explosive transcendental experience. Man encounters God on all the paths of the universe, out of his wondrous yearning for Him: [his encounter with] the natural and the spiritual realms reflecting hidden lights; his experience of freedom within necessity, of the higher realm within the lower one, of the supernatural within the natural; and his feeling of loneliness in a seemingly "Godless" world, Heaven forbid. We might say, paraphrasing a remark of Plotinus, that the lonely one pines for the Lonely One who hides among the shadows. This lonely flesh-and-blood being tries to get the dumb, insensitive world to speak to him. In short, the ontological consciousness, with its movement, purpose, and will, is itself the consciousness of God. Man meets God through questions about the nature of reality, not through abstract logical proofs. He knows, experiences, and lives God because he seeks Him. Man feels God's presence because he has only one question,

"Where is God's glory to be found?" Just as it is impossible to prove that the world exists because the demonstrator is an inseparable part of it, so it is impossible to deduce indirectly that God exists, because He is "the place in which the world has its being" (*Gen. Rabbah* 68:9). He surrounds everything, fills everything, penetrates everything, is within everything, yet is distant from everything. How can the conditioned prove the existence of the One who sets the conditions? However, there is no need for evidence or proof. The very existence of the conditioned testifies to the existence of one setting the conditions. If this is not a complicated logical proof, it is a most certain vision of felt experience. The cultural consciousness peers into an opaque, disjunctive realm which is not its own, and chases after the reflection of the God who oversees everything from the crannies of relative being; it falls in love with the appearance of the handsome lover and follows Him.

≋ Chapter Three

The Disappointed Heart

"Sustain me with raisin cakes, refresh me with
apples, for I am faint with love" (Song 2:5).

A

J udaism knows well the tensions and hesitations involved in
the wearying search for God, as well as the joy and ecstasy of
the search. All the prophets called upon us to observe creation, to
search out the secrets of the cosmic process, to observe the well-
springs of the world, and to uncover the hidden and obscure – the
glory of the Creator's majesty, which hovers over mute creation.
They all wove laurels for the searchers after God, both for those
who seek Him within "mechanical" nature, in its gray opacity,
and for those who tear open the window to the wondrous higher
realms of pure, utterly perfect being. "The heavens declare the
glory of God, the sky proclaims His handiwork" (Ps. 19:2), declares the sweet singer of Israel. "How many are the things You
have made, O Lord; You have made them all with wisdom; the
earth is full of Your creations" (Ps. 104:24), he calls out from the
enthusiasm of the soul, cloaked in the holy spirit, the soul that
yearns for God and beholds a vision of the Almighty. King David views creation primally, seeing the likeness of the Creator reflected in everything, and sings a majestic song. And on the nights

preceding the High Holy Days, when the Jewish people recite their penitential prayers [*selihot*], the beloved clings to her lover and pleads with Him that her request should not be in vain, and that He should present himself to her when she goes out to greet Him. A whispered plea bursts forth and rises with the morning star that appears on the eastern horizon: "Present Yourself to us when we seek You, as it is written, 'And from there you shall seek the Lord your God, and you will find Him if only you seek Him with all your heart and all your soul' [Deut. 4:29]." Master of the universe, behold, we search for and seek You with all our being, we long for You with every beat of our hearts, we run after You. You attract us with an awesome, enormous power that no one can withstand. We hear Your footsteps; You are very, very near to us. Please be here with us now, tonight, the night of penitential prayers, [the night] clothed in secret and mystery, the night of extensive grace and manifold mercies. Please appear when we seek You.

The Halakhah approves of this confrontation between God and man within the world. We are commanded by the Halakhah to utter a benediction over every cosmic phenomenon: over the afterglow of the fiery sunset and the purple of the sunrise trickling along the mountaintops; over the rising moon sprinkling its pale light; over the stars in their courses and the comets leaping from clear space; over the sight of the rainbow in the clouds; over the thunder and lightning arising from mist; over the budding trees and the sweet-smelling exquisite flowers; over the murmur of the ocean and the rushing of the surf; upon eating water and bread, the fruits of the trees and the crops of the fields; over the healthy body, created with wisdom, with its muscles and nerves; over the ability to move and to stand erect. In short, we utter a benediction over everything man encounters that demonstrates the power of creation. What is a benediction – whether *birkat ha-nehenin*, a blessing over something we imbibe, or *birkat re'iyah*, a blessing over something we behold – if not praise and thanksgiving to God for the nature of the world, a nature that changes, in the instant that the benediction is uttered, into a supernatural, miraculous universe; if not the redemption of nature from its muteness, deprivation, and solitude; if not the identification of the cosmic dynamics with the primordial will of the Creator, which is hidden and acts from within its hiding place on organic and inorganic matter, on animal, vegetable, and mineral! What does the benediction attest to if not the strange fact that – in spite of the psychological law that habit and custom dull the subtleties of feeling, dim the alertness of the intellect, and extinguish the flame of ecstasy – the Jew is enthusiastic about each and every phenomenon?

For the Jew there is no such thing as routine. Everything is a wondrous miracle. He is excited by everything, from the novel and unknown to the everyday and the ordinary. In everything he sees the glory of God; over everything he utters a benediction. The beloved goes out always – at each dawn with the radiance of the morning star, and at every twilight with the winking of the evening star, when her drowsy eyelids droop each night and when she opens her eyes every morning – to greet her ruddy lover who peers out from the radiant dawn and the starlight, and from tiredness and rest! The benediction always signifies a moment of grace, a great, sublime moment for the utterer of the benediction, in which he attains a deep vision and acute look through the miraculous portal torn open by a hidden hand to reveal a world that is entirely good and pleasant, and entirely miraculous.[8] The Halakhah says: Fortunate is the creature who encounters the Creator along the pathways of the world from time to time, when he takes a sip of water or tastes a bit of bread. Fortunate is the man for whom God is the Lord whenever he uses his senses and derives enjoyment from them.

Abraham was the first person who sought the God of creation in creation, who observed the reflection of the Creator in the pathways of the universe. It was Abraham who planted a tamarisk in Beersheba and "proclaimed the name of the Lord, God of the world" (Gen. 21:33). The Holy One, Blessed Be He, is present to man in all the phenomena of creation, from the infinitesimal to the great and limitless, from the stem of a lowly plant or a lone tamarisk to the heavenly spaces and astral expanses in which stars are born and ignited, and are also destroyed and extinguished. It was Abraham who commanded his children and household after him to search for the Eternal in time and for the Infinite in the limited and bounded, in accord with the concept of "And let them make Me a sanctuary that I may dwell among them" (Ex. 25:8). It was he who invited weary passersby to refresh themselves in the shade of his tamarisk and told them marvels about the wondrous shade in which man can find perfect, eternal rest.

B

"My beloved had turned and gone" (Song 5:6).

Judaism also knows, however, that this cosmic encounter, despite its importance, greatness, and force, is insufficient. God reveals Himself to His creation, but also eludes it. He is close to us, and the splendor of His majesty breaks forth from every blossoming lily and every ray of light, from the shadows of twilight and the peacefulness of a clear evening filled with expectation and suspense, from the soft breezes of spring and the howling of a storm on a dreary winter night, from the silence of the hills and the quietness of the plain, from the beating of the heart and the rhythmic movements of breathing, from the tumult of the masses and the loneliness of the individual, from the joy of youth and the melancholy of old age. But despite His closeness to us, He is boundlessly far from us. He wraps Himself in a cloud and retires to the recesses of eternity. He lives here with us and also at the "edges" of infinity. Now we see Him, and yet in a moment He rises above us.

The Halakhah knows of the *Shekhinah* revealed, but also of the *Shekhinah* removed. At a time when theologians believed in man's ability to find God within creation, Judaism was not sure of this. According to the Jewish view, man cannot be redeemed from his pollution and contamination, or find his happiness and purpose, by coming close to God through creation alone. Another sort of approach is necessary – an approach through an act of faith. Yearning for God through [contemplating created] reality does not turn into faith. There is experience; but faith is lacking, and Judaism stresses that man needs faith. The distance that separates man from his Creator is infinite; the road from the temporal to the eternal and from the tangible to the transcendent winds through limitless expanses, and man with his limited mind cannot reach his destination. There is an unrealized hint, an unfulfilled aspiration. Indeed, being is pregnant with the *Shekhinah*, and God is revealed through mystery, through that which is incomprehensible in the cosmic process. But what is the nature of this transcendental realm that peers out from its recesses? It is the unveiling of the incomprehensible absolute, which winks an eye and disappears. It is the revelation of eternity, whose image cannot be recorded in our limited consciousness. There is a revelation of God as an unsolvable riddle. Man encounters a principle that is above nature, a reality set apart from the ontic drama, a reality that is the source and purpose of tangible existence.

Man's achievement, however, is not clear. Man has discovered something that is separate from the world, but he does not know what it is. How can a finite mind understand the infinite? How can the temporal mind perceive the eternal? The theologian in this context cannot comprehend the essence of the absolute and eternal except through the use of negative attributes [attributes that are understood as expressing what God is not]. The absolute is totally different from the contingent world, and there is nothing in common between the Creator and anything in His creation. The representatives of a rational, cosmic religiosity, who began with tangible reality and ended with the experience of the absolute and eternal, were not able to formulate their conclusions in a positive, logical way that would satisfy the man of God who is seeking his Creator. They struggled with man's yearning and thirst for God, but they did not prevail.

The truth of the matter is, finding the absolute through being involves the use of abstraction. When man abstracts the universal from the particulars and empties his conception of the whole variegated spectrum of particularity, with all its changes and transformations, he attains a single general idea that encompasses the pinnacle of being. But this concept, which has been abstracted from the freshness and variety of the concrete, turns into a hollow idea lacking content and bereft of the abundance of the individual essence. There is a general conception that has neither the rich variety nor the majestic beauty of existence. What is pure form in Aristotle's view? In its role as the supreme concept of being and the prime mover of the world, its negativity is greater than its positivity! What is the hidden One of Plotinus if not the incomprehensible "beyond," devoid of any particular essence, which cannot be given any title, not even that of First Cause? The transcendental silence of the abyss surrounds everything for the Greek philosophers; in their view, a barren wasteland of simple unity, with nothingness peering out of it, extends over everything. This is the Absolute, Lonely One who creates the living, variegated, stormy being through gradual derivation.

Essentially, rational cosmic religiosity devolves into pantheism – whether that of Plotinus and his emanations or that of Benedict Spinoza and his substance with infinite attributes. Their common denominator is that they are but a single step away from atheism. In a word, if religiosity derives its substance only from the intellect and cultural consciousness, it leads to denial of God. This truth was known to R. Judah Halevi, when he said that the God of Aristotle was to be found in abstraction and generalization, "and apprehended via syllogism" (*Kuzari* IV:15).

Moreover, even this abstract achievement does not last long within culture. Just as blue flames burst out of the darkness of a gloomy night, far away at the ends of the mysterious horizon, and then die away in an instant, so too does the spark of divinity flicker in the mists of reality. And just as the rainbow in the sky quickly vanishes, so does the image of God as reflected in the thick clouds of being. He who relies only on the cosmological approach will end up ruined and faithless. Just look at the heretical movements that denied God and turned everything on its head. These movements were never merely movements; they were not formed haphazardly. They appear in every age, in every generation. They stem from insanity, from the pride and madness of the mind.

However, the world itself, with its strange qualities, is also to blame for the human confusion that leads people to dissidence and rebellion. Scientists see the world as enveloped in an abundance of formal lawfulness; positivists see it as full of dim, thick sensuousness. Both of these conceal the secret of creation. The [scientific] symbolic husk and the [positivist's] perceptible husk form a barrier between man and the Creator. Sometimes the construction created by the mind is perceived as an absolute entity and is maintained as a total solution to the eternal problem. Man's pride and impudence drive him to deify himself as the solution to the mystery. Then the scientist goes mad and denies God. At other times, it is the sensuous quality, in its powerful primitivity, that seizes the center of man's consciousness and blocks his path toward God. Then the hedonist goes mad and denies God.

Seeking God only within existence is a daring and risky adventure, which sometimes meets up with threatened failure. Although, in moments of inspiration, people do hear the sound of the Lord moving about in the garden of being, these moments are ephemeral and quickly pass. The echo fades away and is swallowed up in the expanses of the Infinite. Love-stricken Being searches for her lover, but does not find Him. There is a powerful experience of God here, but it is manifested within the limitations and restrictions of human cognitive ability and through its clash with the mystery. A bold attempt of this sort – revealing the *Shekhinah* within nature, with all nature's glory and greatness, but without going outside nature – does not bring man closer to God. The end result of the effort at revealing God in the realm of being, using cognitive stratagems, is spiritual weariness and bankruptcy. "Understanding Him means wearying of the aim of understanding

Him" (Maimonides, *Guide of the Perplexed*, 1:59 [reflecting the Ibn Tibbon Hebrew translation]).

The beloved seeks her lover, but He eludes her.[9]

C

Why is man unable to find his Creator as he seeks and pursues Him to the ends of the cosmos, which is stamped with God's primordial will? The cause of man's frustration in this area is sin, which separates him from his Creator. If not for sin, man would be able to reveal the Creator in the creation without any disappointment. Then he would see God's glory filling the universe and would sense that the regal splendor and majesty of the surrounding world emanate from the Infinite; then he would be aware of the presence of the *Shekhinah* in every growing blade of grass and every flowing stream. Our rabbis said, "The essence of the *Shekhinah* is in the lower world" (*Gen. Rabbah* 19:7). The world was created not in order to humiliate and pain man, but for the sake of God's glory and goodness, so that He could reveal Himself to humans and become intimate with them. But the serpent pounced upon Adam and beguiled him to do wrong and to sin. As a result of this sin, the *Shekhinah* removed itself from the lower world. "They heard the sound of the Lord God moving about in the garden in the wind of the day" (Gen. 3:8). The Holy One, Blessed Be He, left the garden, which is the world. The *Shekhinah* went into exile from the lower world to the recesses of eternity and infinity, to the upper heavens. A fixed husk of mechanistic consciousness covers the inwardness of the living world that sings songs of praise to its Creator; it covers the soul and inner core of the creation. We certainly believe that at some time in the future, when tears are wiped from exhausted faces and evil is eradicated forever, the throne of God's honor will become firmly established in the lower world, and all creatures will know that it was God who created them, that they are God's handiwork. At the present time, however, God is hiding Himself from us because of sin, and all human efforts to reveal God within creation end in failure and frustration.

Even now, God is *mekomo shel olam*, the "place" of the universe, and there is no location that is devoid of Him; but this presence cannot be seen or experienced. The Holy One, Blessed Be He, sees but is not seen. He descends into the world in a pillar of cloud, whose thickness no human being can penetrate. When man begins to come closer to God because he hears the sound of God moving in the expanse of the universe, God draws away from him. As described above, finite man and the Infinite seek but cannot find each other. This dialectical drama is revealed in all its force and majesty. Man remains lonely. Who can redeem him from his loneliness if not the God Who is hiding from him?

Chapter Four

The Surprised Heart

"I am asleep, but my heart is wakeful.
Hark, my beloved knocks!" (Song 5:2).

A

*T*he lover seeks His beloved, His beautiful one. The Creator seeks the creature, the spiritual personality; He knocks at the opening of the tent and whispers with a lover's passion: "Let me in, my sister, my darling, my faultless dove..." (Song 5:2).

As described above, man's search for God expresses itself in intellectual activity. All sapient men search for God, but when the seekers reach the ultimate boundary of reality they become alarmed and retreat. When they confront eternity, with its terrifying spaces that both attract and repel, both encourage and mock – they all cease their journey. Many of them are confused; many are frightened and uproot their faith. Only a few remain steadfast in the face of the mystery and expect salvation from the God they seek. This is the crisis point, and here God reveals Himself from above nature, from beyond the world bounded by time and space.

God reveals Himself to His creation above and beyond nature, bringing prophecies to human beings. This is the new Torah that was given at Sinai to slaves who had become free, and who then gave it to the rest of the world. God reveals Himself to man in the desert: "He found him in a desert region, in an empty howling waste. He engirded him, watched over him, guarded him like the apple of His eye" (Deut. 32:10). Not in a settled, flourishing land, but on the plains of a great and terrible desert – a wasteland in the shadow of death – does God appear from among the holy myriads. At a time when it seems as if man has ceased searching for God in the desolate wasteland, and has given up on everything, God reveals Himself to man.

This revelation is not a reply to man's questions and doubts, visions and longings. The sight of God is not a response to human yearning. God arrives suddenly when He thinks of revealing Himself. Man does not and cannot know when or why. God surprises man, who is not expecting salvation and is not mad with longing or burdened with the mystery of creation. The Deity encounters flesh-and-blood individuals who are satisfied with the manifest and the superficial, who confine themselves within the pale, yellowing, desolate husk of existence. When the tempest is under control, when the desire to search is ended, when the heart is dulled and the soul frozen, and the entire universe is dying in a deep nightmarish sleep, then God emerges from His isolation and secrecy and reveals Himself to man.

The exposure of the Hidden One to a world of chaos because that is His will – this is the revelation of the *Shekhinah*. God revealed Himself to Adam when he had sunk into the deep mire of the original sin that had separated him from his Creator and was not expecting a revelation of the *Shekhinah*. The Israelites leave Egypt – as slaves captivated by the fleshpots and all their delicacies, who have not yet rid themselves of the filth of servitude nor have yet shaken the brick dust off their faces – and God reveals Himself in the third month after the Exodus. They sin with the golden calf and betray the Husband of their youth, and the Holy One, Blessed Be He, comes down in a cloud from the heavenly plains and stands with Moses. God initially reveals Himself to man at a time of growing evil in the world, when the splendor of life and the vision of a holiness-filled existence have departed. God's first words to man come at a time of historical and metaphysical desolation. When a torrent of despair is about to quench all the aspirations of the distressed and yearning soul, when no dolorous confessions break out of the suffering heart, when no prayerful cry goes up to God – then God reveals Himself.

B

This is Judaism's view. God reveals Himself to man when he is in the grip of a fate cruel as vultures, bereft of hope or vision. The encounter with God to forestall the expulsion of man from God's inheritance, the Creator revealing Himself to the creature who is suspended over the abyss – this is the secret of the revelation of the *Shekhinah*. A lofty existence breaks forth and rises from ontological negation, planting comes in the wake of uprooting, and destruction opens the door to redemption. Bricks and straw, the oppression and suffering of the people, the inanity and ugliness of life – all lead to the revelation of the *Shekhinah*.

The general theologian's approach, by contrast, is strewn with roses and adorned with grace. It finds what it wants in the image of *Logos* [reason] and the figure of *Nous* [mind], in pure form, in ideas gloriously displayed, in the inherent harmony of the world's regulation. From the lawful, the regulated, the good, and the beautiful, the general theologian ascends to the absolute, the perfect, and the One. But philosophical theology is perplexed and confused when it encounters impermanence, disorder, evil, negativity, privation, and formlessness. Therefore the later Greek philosophers concluded that matter is the source of all the evil and chaos in the world, and they believed – Heaven forbid – that matter is outside God's domain. Out of their abysmal confusion and black despair at the sight of evil, the "chaos" of reality, they made use of dualism to "justify" and to "explain" the hell and sorrow in life.

Authentic Jewish thought, rooted in faith in the absolute creation *ex nihilo*, introduced a mutual relationship between God and man. First, man searches for God through reason, ordered and il-luminated by the splendor of the great, magnificent creation. This search is expressed in the poem of creation, "Bless, my soul, the Lord" (Psalm 104). Man finds his God in the splendor and glory of the world, the abundance of radiances, the myriads of captivating sights, motion and action, power, the static and the dynamic, the greatness and might in the cosmic drama. From this experience of the divine there bursts forth, as stated above, a formula for benedictions that expresses thanksgiving and praise for a proper existence in a fine, lawful world. These benedictions refer to the magnificent, stable cosmic process. Man must be grateful to the Creator for His continuous creation, directed by the primordial will of necessity.

God, too, seeks man through the obscure and incomprehensible, when the creature is swept away in the maelstrom of a mad reality and "wild" happenings that are unexplainable and inconceivable, so that man stands agape, waiting to know that which cannot be known. Out of the black agony of man's standing before the arcane riddle of the evil in the world, God reveals Himself. "When I passed by you and saw you wallowing in your blood, I said to you: In your blood live!" (Ezek. 16:6). "One must utter a blessing over misfortunes just as one utters a blessing over good events" (*Mishnah Berakhot* 9:5), and one must love God for whatever measure He metes out. "'You shall love the Lord your God... with all your soul' (Deut. 6:5) – even when He takes your soul" (*Sifrei* 32). Even when harsh judgment is meted out, and man cannot understand its nature or its essence, God is being revealed. Even out of negativity and obscurity the True Judge comes forth.

Halakhic thought wonders about evil not from a metaphysical standpoint, but from a moral-halakhic perspective. It does not ask why or from what cause, but for what purpose. It is interested not in the causal aspect, but in the teleological element of evil. Its question is a halakhic one: What should man do when confronted by evil, so that he may live and flourish? How can we turn evil into a creative force? How can evil be used to enhance the rule of the good? The Jew first accepts the judgment and then fights the evil, conquers it, and elevates it to the level of the good. The reply to evil is repentance. Out of his suffering, man raises himself up and returns to God: "When you are in distress because all these things have befallen you, in the end of days, you shall return to the Lord your God and obey Him" (Deut. 4:30). Suffering obliges man to repent. The response to "distress" is the act of repentance.

C

Let us now recapitulate, presenting some examples of this idea from the Bible and rabbinic sources. God's revelation at times of crisis, from the depths of despair and distress, is a basic principle of Judaism. Sometimes God does not reveal Himself to the contented soul; He reveals Himself to the mute soul, battered by weariness and exertion. Sometimes God reveals Himself to one who grieves for the ruin of His Temple and the destruction of its altars, while avoiding one who dedicates His Temple and stands at the side of his offering; sometimes He does not reveal Himself to the rational individual, but to one who is confused about life, who is bankrupt and has lost track of his world. From time to time, man's salvation comes out of distress.

Even the choicest members of the Jewish people first encountered their Lord at a time of raging fear, helplessness, and distraction, when they were not anticipating such an encounter but were thoroughly surprised by it. Jacob comes close to his God in a nocturnal dream, while sleeping on the cold "stones of that place" (Gen. 28:11). Moses encounters a burning bush at a time when he is pasturing Jethro's flock, entirely devoted to this simple everyday occupation (Ex. 3:1–2). Ezekiel sees visions of God in exile, on the river Kebar, at a time when the appearance of the present, full of quaking and horror, contradicts the vision of a glorious future (Ezek. 1:1).

Judaism has firmly established the halakhic principle that even when man confronts an unchangeable evil decree coming from God, when his rejected prayers are thrown back in his face, he must see God and conjoin with Him in spite of the tragic reality that weighs him down. God reveals Himself through suffering and tragedy, when the individual or the community are in trouble and distress. Moses pleads with God, but his prayer is not accepted (Deut. 3:23–28). His destined fate turns into a fate without destiny. He sees the chosen land, but he cannot go there. The divine attribute of justice indicts him and seals the gates of heaven before him. Precisely out of the pain and torment, out of the affliction and suffering, the kiss of God suddenly appears, detaching Moses from this world and bringing him to a world full of goodness and light. Saul at Gilgal, powerless, deprived of his royal future and messianic vision, surrenders to the prophet of rage and bows down before his God (1 Sam. 15:31). His coat is torn, his heart is rent apart, his kingdom is split, his sorrow is overwhelming. The pain of a world whose foundations have toppled pierces his heart, yet he nevertheless is faithful to God and keeps his eyes trustfully directed toward Him. R. Akiva turns himself over to God even when historical reality buffets and mocks him (*Berakhot* 61b). He masters his raging cry and his tears, and recites the *Shema* in a passion of longing and yearning.

D

When man wants to avoid God's revelation, God seizes him; God closes in on him and there is no escape. If the creature attempts to run away and escape from the great, awesome God, God pursues him. "Adam and his wife hid from the Lord God" (Gen. 3:8); "…when the people saw it, they fell back and stood at a distance. 'You speak to us,' they said to Moses, 'and we will obey; but let not God speak to us, lest we die'" (Ex. 20:15–16); "…the men who were with me did not see the vision, yet they were seized with great terror and fled into hiding" (Dan. 10:7). At times man fears God and runs away from Him, but God overtakes him. He hides, and God seeks him. God overtakes man when he is in distress, when man tries to elude Him; when the captive strives to loosen the bonds of the Absolute and remove its yoke, he falls wallowing in his failure. Jonah tried to escape but did not succeed. With the revelation of the *Shekhinah*, the tension between finitude and infinity is revealed. The creature is weighed down by the burden of eternity, and when he rebels, his rebellion is in vain. When God reveals Himself to man, He does so not in order to realize an intellectual, scientific goal – to tell him about the cosmic drama – but to command him and to give him the responsibility for keeping laws and statutes, positive and negative commandments. The God of Sinai is the God of the Will, the Inscrutable One who commands us to follow a unique way of life without explaining why or for what purpose. The God of creation is the God of the Hidden Intellect who created everything in His wisdom without satisfying our curiosity and without explaining His acts – the creation. The All-knowing and the All-willing are two of God's attributes.

When man seeks God, he is seeking an intellect that is beyond him. He wants this intellect to take note of him and to enlighten him about the universe, about the essence and fate of man, but instead of finding the Hidden Intellect, he encounters the Inscrutable Will. This Will reveals itself to man, and instead of telling him the secrets of creation, it demands unlimited discipline and absolute submission. This infinite, all-powerful Will places man in a state of subjugation from which there is no release; it compels the finite to surrender to it and obey it forever. The Hidden Intellect encourages the creature and comforts him in his affliction. The Inscrutable Will conquers and subdues him. The Revealed Will does not brook any opposition. Man appears as absolutely subordinate, as receiving the commandments and bending under the weight of his burden. The acceptance of the command does not contain any feeling of freedom. It is composed entirely of compulsion. "He placed the mountain over them like a barrel and said, 'If you accept the Torah, well and good; if not, this will be your grave'" (*Shabbat* 88a). There is no refuge from God; He demands of man absolute submission.

E

In this realm, prophecy appears as the discourse of the Creator to the created without any attachment between God and man. The discourse does not remove God's absolute separateness; God reveals Himself to man and commands him, but the divine withdrawal is not abrogated. God appears beyond existence. On the contrary, the awareness of the abyss between God and man is heightened, and man is aware of his inability to cleave to God. The only link between them is the revelational discourse, and it too, as mentioned, is one-way: God speaking to man to give him commandments.

The awareness of revelation, as noted above, is manifested mainly in a fearful experience, a sense that the order of reality has been conquered by an awesome transcendent power that cannot be grasped by the mind. This awareness is filled with a strange secrecy and an amazing supra-rationality. "Fear and trembling came upon me, causing all my bones to quake with fright. A wind passed by me, making the hair of my flesh bristle. It halted; its appearance was strange to me; a form loomed before my eyes; I heard a murmur, a voice," relates Eliphaz the Temanite about his night visions (Job 4:14–16). This is the sense of the presence of an unrecognizably awesome figure, the sense of the silence of a night of horror and torment; and out of the silence a voice is heard. Fright envelops the one who sees. An obscure dimness covers everything, and out of the dimness the Infinite reveals itself. "So I was left alone to see this great vision; I was drained of strength, my vigor was destroyed, and I could not summon up strength," recounts Daniel (10:8). The vision is accompanied by the fearful trembling of the poor, lonely individual encountering an awesome conquering force. Even the father of our nation, with whom God walked, stoops under the weight of the revelation and is alarmed by the darkness of the dread that leaps upon him in the vision of the *berit bein ha-betarim,* the Covenant between the Parts: "As the sun was about to set... a great dark dread descended upon him

[Abraham]" (Gen. 15:12). The clear day, a symbol of rational existence, had disappeared, and the dread-laden dark night had arrived. The great vision became a mystery, a transfinite secret that cannot be fathomed.

ઊ Chapter Five

The Yearning Yet Fearful Heart

"'But,' He said, 'you cannot see My face, for man
may not see Me and live'" (Ex. 33:20).

A

God's revelation to man, which occurred at Mount Sinai and on other occasions to privileged individuals who were chosen by Providence to be His prophets, became for posterity a perpetual experience, a unique awareness. In all generations, man lives and feels this revelation the way he lives and feels a natural longing for God. We are commanded about this in the portion *Va-Ethanan* (Deut. 4:9–10): "But take utmost care and watch yourselves scrupulously, lest you forget the things that you saw with your own eyes and so that they do not fade from your heart as long as you live. And make them known to your children and to your children's children: The day you stood before the Lord your God at Horeb... " We are warned not to forget two things: (1) the laws and statutes that God commanded us at Horeb; (2) the experience of divine revelation, of standing before God with all the fear and trembling that accompany man's confrontation with the Infinite. We are commanded to sense the revelation in all its awe and grandeur as if we had just now returned to our tents from our encounter with God at Sinai, as if we had just witnessed the thunder and lightning and felt a very great dread. This remembrance is not mechanical or associative. Rather, it is a tremendously powerful vital remembrance, an all-encompassing and all-penetrating consciousness. It thus appears that there is a duality in man's approach to the Creator. This duality is manifested in a twofold consciousness: a natural, ontological one and a prophetic, revelatory one.

The meaning of "natural consciousness" is this. On the one hand, man's spirit soars to great distances. There is an aspiration rooted in our spiritual being to direct all the multiplicity in our limited temporal reality toward the First, non-contingent Existent, who acts within and beyond the world. On the other hand, there is a universe impressed with the Creator's stamp which offers a hint of a transcendent reality. In this framework, man's experience of the world is, in its essence and its purpose, the experience of God, the world's Creator. The initiative must be human; man must seek God.

The meaning of "revelational consciousness" is this. Man cannot come to God on his own, through the initiative of his own spirit; the world is a dead end which does not permit passage to the realm of the eternal and the absolute. Man's spirit soaring up to the heavens, propelled by massive jolts and fiery longing, reaches only the shadow of the Almighty, the image of His image; she will never rest in God's bosom and cling to her lover. Therefore God revealed Himself to human beings and said to them, "I am the Lord your God" (Ex. 20:2). A truth of this sort, says the revelational consciousness, will never be exhausted by human reason. The very vision of the awesome, incomprehensible revelation takes place against man's will and without his consent. On the contrary, man fears the penetration of the unfathomable into his simple world and covers his face.

Judaism espouses this rift in the religious consciousness. On the one hand, as I have pointed out, Jewish sages have never denied man's initiative to seek God or the noetic nature of human longing for Him. This [noetic] longing partakes of some of the deepest cognition and some of the loftiest experience of the truth. At times, there is even a parallel between religion and reason. Man is commanded not only to believe in God, but also to know God, as Maimonides formulated the first commandment: "to know that there is a First Existent who brought every existing thing into being" (Laws of the Foundations of the Torah 1:1). The meaning of "knowledge" is knowing God by knowing His works – the works of creation. Yet, on the other hand, our sages insisted that knowing God through nature is insufficient. The paramount principle is faith in His revelation to man, and readiness to fulfill His will unconditionally. Man seeks God and is also a captive of God. This duality gives a special, original content to the religious experience advocated by our Torah. Thus it was the primordial will of the Creator to plant two sorts of consciousness in man – a dual-faceted approach.[10]

B

What is a religious experience? On the one hand, it is an experience which includes the development of the individual's spirit. It is a cognitive and moral as well as an aesthetic experience; it elevates its subject to the height of ontological consciousness, irrespective of the various theories regarding the origin of religious activity. This state of mind is woven within the creative spirit and intertwined with all its threads and fibers. From this viewpoint, religious consciousness is manifested as the consciousness of absolute freedom. Man seeks God out of a thirst for the freedom of life, a desire to expand and deepen the universe. The search for God means liberation from the burden of tyrannical nature weighing heavily upon him, release from the blind forces besetting man's life. Weary from the travail of dull life, man flees to the region of complete liberty and conjoins with God. Man desires peace of mind and seeks to wipe the tears of sorrow from his face. Out of the totality of spiritual experience that flows from the inner uniqueness and independence of the creative spirit that rises ever higher, the religious experience is revealed. When the person who longs for God arrives at the border of the absolute and the eternal, he does not feel any compulsive force. On the contrary, he voluntarily soars into the heavens and seeks the traces of the One who dwells there. The creature needs the refuge of charity, mercy, total salvation, and the redemption of existence. The more he breaks through the curtain dividing him from his God, the more his freedom will grow and the more intensely will his joy in existence pour forth.

Religious experience, in this context, is the outbreak of the wondrous force of the spontaneous metaphysical spirit in all its colorful variety and raging activity – a partnership in the act of creation. It leaps out of its restricted circle, aspires to the pinnacle of being with the enthusiasm of victory and sweeping triumph, viewing distant horizons reddening in the dawn of infinity. This sort of flourishing religiosity "shines through like the dawn" that drips on the mountaintops immersed in the morning dew; it is "beautiful as the moon" in the quiet night filled with serene breezes, and "radiant as the sun" in a transparently blue sky on a clear autumn day (see Song 6:10). The paramount principle is that man knows that religious life is an indivisible part of his essence; that the act is free, drawing its strength from his innermost being. All his spiritual directions – theoretical, ethical, and aesthetic – come together in a perfect variegated unity. The contents of his thought, will, and emotion are blended in the revelation of the religious sensibility. Man was created in God's image. A spark of the Creator was hidden in him. He desires creative freedom. The religious experience enables him to achieve this desire.

The revelational faith experience, unlike the natural ontological experience, is unrelated to the spirit of the free, creative human being and does not involve the aspirations of cultural creation in all its varied developments. The revelational experience is a realm unto itself, surrounded by barriers, and not available to man's conception. The creative force of the *logos* and the *ethos* does not apply to this type of consciousness. On the contrary, from time to time there are clashes between the two types of consciousness or experience – the revelational and the natural. In contrast to the more tolerant natural consciousness, revelational religion lusts for unrestricted control [over man]. It cannot tolerate the sharing of authority or the blending of realms ("Anyone who joins the name of Heaven with any other thing is removed from the world" [*Sukkah* 45b]). Sometimes it refuses to couple with cultural life or live together with it. It aspires to encompass all of man's being and fill all of its essence.

The fundamental principle is that revelational consciousness is not a continuation of cultural consciousness and does not identify with it. It stands alone and is not swept away in the stream of cultural consciousness. Its image is characterized by closure and separation. Its nature is aboriginal, its essence incomprehensible. It is the consciousness of the revelation of the *Shekhinah*, the imposition of authority on the powerless creature. It is the consciousness of necessity and subjugation; it is an absolute awareness of the revealed duty that preempts man's will. It is distinct from the awareness of natural moral duties, which is rooted in the general consciousness that yearns for total freedom. In the field of revelational experience, man accepts the yoke of the commandments against his will and subordinates his pride and self-love to God.

C

Rational religious experience also differs from revelational experience in the way it develops. The former develops in the directions in which human cultural values take shape. At its height, it is an idea embodied in the achievements of the spirit that rend the heavens. It is the most radiant and brilliant thread in the frame of mind of cultured man, who is mobile and whose image is changeable. Thus, it too embodies vital motion, fascination, and constant renewal. The horizons are breathtaking, drenched in glory. Infinity and finitude meet, time and eternity touch. As science progresses, so does man's knowledge of God as His Creator, as the One who endows man with reason. When man reveals new foundations of knowledge that explain natural phenomena which were not understood before, his rational religious experience is deepened.

God created humanity as male and female, and He commanded them to master the world: "fill the earth and subdue it" (Gen. 1:28). How can a human being master the world, or even some part of it, if not by grasping the laws of nature and using them for man's benefit? Scientific progress is part of man's destiny in the world that the Creator of the universe fashioned for us.

However, natural religious consciousness is itself part of this blessing. Man's mastery of the world, of the environment, cannot be complete until man realizes that the mathematical laws of physics contain within themselves the primordial will of the Creator. For the Creator is present here, nearby, very near to us – and also there, far away, very far from us. Man's mission cannot be completed merely by revealing the mechanical order of the universe; dry knowledge cannot save man. Only the combination of scientific reason with the heart that searches and yearns for the living God can allow man to progress. It is for this reason that God made man a scientific creature, able to understand the truth, and at the same time an individual who longs for God and is capable of transcending the shackles of science.

The second sort of consciousness is altogether different. This aspect of religious consciousness is, as mentioned, unique – the awareness of a compulsory covenant, submission and acceptance of the yoke of the Kingdom of Heaven. One who lives the vision of the revelation of the *Shekhinah* stands beyond the authority of the cultured creative mind that is subject to change and alteration. He is entirely engulfed in an astonishing, alien zone, devoid of spiritual development and renewal. Everything here persists, everything remains in existence with a stable identity. Novelty, which is one of the wonders of temporality, does not apply to something revelational that emanates from the bosom of eternity. Development and revealed faith are antithetical concepts. "Faith" means an act that is explainable, not through the stream of natural consciousness, but through the revelation of the *Shekhinah* to man and man's joining an eternal world that is entirely stable, persistent, and without transformation or novelty. In truth, the man of faith sometimes divests himself of his cultural treasures and the rule of metamorphosis. The revelational form of life, with its firmly embedded principles, forces the spirit to check its powerful course. Culture flows on, continually taking on new forms, sweeping up natural religion in its eddies; revelational faith overcomes the transitory, jealously guarding its eternal persistence. It is entirely given over to transcendental necessity and is expressed in an eternal formulation. It is all lingering, repose, and quiet. The wonder of repose, within a world full of motion and alteration, is found in the revelational experience. Any act of repair or change of values in the realm of revelational faith saps its original strength, and its benefits are outweighed by its deficiencies.

❧ Chapter Six
The Divided Heart

"Thy heart shall fear, and be enlarged" (Isa. 60:5).

A

This schism, which has sunk deep into the transcendental consciousness, involves an eternal antinomy that envelops the experience of God. Judaism gives it a wondrous name: the attribute of mercy and the attribute of justice.

What is the attribute of mercy?

God is a merciful deity, in whose bosom man finds absolute good and happiness. Man's aspiration for God is essentially the yearning of the lonely individual, bereft of peace of mind or joy, for happiness and repose. The individual – storm-tossed, sunk in the depths of secular life, with little purpose or meaning, full of denial and panic – runs to God as to a safe refuge, to quiet and repose, where he will be liberated from his mute suffering. Death stalks him, nihility hunts him; the creation, out of an indifference that is sometimes clothed in the guise of terrifying hatred, shows him a taunting visage, mocks his heart's desires, derides his lofty hopes and frustrates his initiatives. In the universe, grief exceeds joy, disappointment dominates over fulfillment, opacity overcomes illumination and understanding. Man wishes to triumph over death, to turn senseless fate into a spiritual destiny with a clear direction, and to achieve both a joyful temporal existence and eternal life. He yearns for God so as to take shelter under His wings and repose in His shadow, where he will find what His heart desires.

This longing is mainly pragmatic, born of the instinct to continue one's biological existence that is implanted in man as a living creature. This vital natural instinct finds its expression in man's running toward God. Indeed, these yearnings redeem the instinct from its subordination to indifferent nature and elevate it to a sublime spiritual height, for man finds the fulfillment of his instinctual yearning in a realm beyond the material world by coming closer to God as a spiritual being. The aspiration itself is, nevertheless, a vital instinctual one emanating from man's animal nature. Natural man seeks preservation, while spiritual man reveals the secret of preservation to natural man: where it can be found, and what it is. He tells him that his preservation depends upon his rising above the self. The instinct for self-preservation takes the form of the spiritual person's moral flight toward God. Man runs toward the transitory life, *hayyei sha'ah*, and finds eternal life, *hayyei olam*.

"Like a hind yearning for water brooks, my soul yearns for You, O God" (Ps. 42:2). The longing of the deer for a stream of water and the longing of the soul for its lover both stem from the same natural, vital instincts. Burning thirst drives the deer to the brook, and the instinctive yearning for existence drives the human being to God. The hind slakes its thirst in the cascading waters of the stream, while the soul slakes its own thirst by running toward God. The love for God embodied in this longing is a selfish love, a love for the reward involved in becoming closer to God: the conquest of man's fear. "The Lord is my shepherd; I lack nothing.... Though I walk through the valley of the shadow of death I fear no harm, for You are with me" (Ps. 23:1, 4). The terror of the shadow of death and the desire for repose draw man toward God. At this stage, man is still unaware of the demand that accompanies his drawing closer to God, namely, to follow a particular way of life; he is unaware of the commandments. In this state, man is unafraid and unworried that God may dictate, demand, force, reprove, and punish. He sees God only as the merciful Father embracing His son and granting him a wealth of kisses showing love and special affection.

B

What is the attribute of justice?

God appears to man as the King of judgment, awesome and terrifying. He is the fire that consumes fire (see *Yoma* 21b), the judge and punisher; His sparks are flames, His seal is truth, and His attribute is justice. He demands of man self-sacrifice, utter subordination, and fulfillment of the commandments. One who comes close to God will be brought to trial for negligence and sloth, for a life filled with rebellion and folly. Woe is the man who is found guilty! God finds fault everywhere, even in those who are fashioned of clay. In this situation, when man encounters the attribute of justice, a terrible fear overtakes him. He despairs and attempts to flee. He thinks, as did Adam, that his existence depends on fleeing from the King of judgment, not on running toward Him. Man thinks that his existence depends on extending his fear of God, rather than extending his love for Him, for who can be found righteous before His tribunal? This fear, which causes anxiety-filled retreat, is a fear of total annihilation. When God is the prosecutor, how can man appear before Him as the defendant? The helpless defendant has no right to stand before the mighty and powerful prosecutor, who is respected and feared by all who surround Him. The feeling of fear of God, like the yearning for Him, belongs to the natural realm, and is rooted in the instinctive reaction of living creatures to outbursts of power – to eliminate the threat that endangers their existence. Once again, the yearning is natural and instinctive, while its fulfillment is spiritual. Natural man, driven by animal panic, "flees" from God, and by this "flight" he becomes spiritual man, for he serves God in this flight by experiencing terrible fear. Out of the fear is revealed the revelational awareness and the decision to fulfill God's will.

"For the Lord of Hosts has ready a day against all that is proud…, against all that is lofty – so that it is brought low… then man's haughtiness shall be humbled and the pride of man brought low. None but the Lord shall be exalted in that day" (Isa. 2:12, 17). Man flees from God: "And men shall enter caverns in the rock and hollows in the ground – before the terror of the Lord and His dread majesty, when He comes forth to overcome the earth" (Isa. 2:19). God, who reveals Himself out of His utter separation as a *mysterium tremendum*, an awesome mystery, walks terrifyingly with the despicable "small creature, lowly and obscure, endowed with slight and slender intelligence, standing in the presence of Him who is perfect in knowledge" (Maimonides, *Mishneh Torah*, Laws of the Foundations of the Torah 2:2). This tiny creature flees out of utter despair.[11]

≈ Chapter Seven

The Heart That Runs and Flees

*"And when the people saw it, they retreated
and stood at a distance." (Ex. 20:15).*

A

*H*alakhah gives its approval to this antithetical experience. Both trust and fear are necessary for religious consciousness. Looking toward God out of the expectation of reward is acceptable; and awe of God resulting from hovering anxiety is also essential to this consciousness. Our sages said, "One should always engage in the [study of] Torah and [the fulfillment of] the commandments [even if] not for their own sake, because [engagement] not for their own sake will lead to [engagement] for their own sake" (*Pesahim* 50b, *Sotah* 22b); "Serve [God] out of fear, so that if you feel like rebelling, know that you fear, and one who fears does not rebel" (*Midrash Tanna'im*, Deut. 6:5); "[If one says, 'I am giving] this coin to charity so that my son will live,' this is a completely righteous act" (*Pesahim* 8a, *Rosh ha-Shanah* 4a). The awareness of the revelational responsibility inheres in the awareness of the punishment meted out to one who sins. The difference between fear of God and fear of punishment is merely terminological. Commandments require intention, but this intention is concentrated in the awareness of one's obligation and of the fulfillment of the divine will.

With the reader's permission I will add a few remarks. The fact that the antithetical experience of love and fear – of the desire to run toward God and the desire to run away from Him – is rooted deep in our biological nature and in the situation of man as a psychosomatic creature does not make this experience any the less valuable or significant. Halakhah has always dealt with real human existence, restraining it with the awareness of reward and punishment, without seeing any defect in man's will to exist in the biological sense, to enjoy his existence to the fullest, and to be free of physical or psychological pain. For this reason, Halakhah restrains man with the promise of reward and punishment and gives him the choice between the blessing and the curse. The blessing is the good in the natural life, and the curse is the dominion of evil in it. In order to subjugate him to the supernatural revelational command, the Halakhah both frightens and reassures natural man.

Even the greatest figures of the Jewish people experienced the dread of punishment in all its intensity. R. Yohanan ben Zakkai cried before his death. When his disciples asked him why he was crying, he responded that he feared the King of Kings, who exists eternally and whose anger and punishment are eternal (*Berakhot* 28b). This fear, with all its force, pervades exalted people who have reached the supreme degree of perfection and who have served their Creator on a very sublime level. Fear and trust are together the background of the religious life; without them no religiosity can exist. It is with good reason that Maimonides defined the commandment of fearing God, in his *Book of the Commandments*, as the fear of punishment (positive commandment 4). We have already mentioned that the Halakhah sets down a special commandment of repentance in times of trouble: "When you are in distress... you shall return to the Lord your God" (Deut. 4:30), "and if you go to war in your land... then you shall blow an alarm with the trumpets... and you shall be saved from your enemies"

(Num. 10:9). Whatever distresses man obligates him to repent. All the commandments regarding fast days, such as blowing the trumpets, crying out in prayer, and avoiding bodily pleasures, constitute the details of one central commandment: repentance out of the distress that the attribute of justice has brought down upon man. Once more, the fear bursts forth out of the depths of man's natural existence and vitality, from deep desires that aspire to real physical existence. This voiceless fear brings man to a miraculous ascension to the level of the individual possessed of spirit and vision. As R. Solomon Ibn Gabirol wrote in *Keter Malkhut* (sec. 38): "If You seek my sins, I will run away from You toward You, and I will hide from Your anger in Your shade."

B

Although both of these approaches – the natural one with its yearning for God and the revelational one with its fear and withdrawal – begin in the realm of emotional religious experience far removed from any moral or practical motifs, these motifs are in the end reflected in the moral-practical orientation of the man of God. The attitude of individuals who seek God out of their longing for complete spiritual freedom is totally different from that of individuals who recoil when God reveals Himself to them. The religious personality who is torn between the two aspects is liable to come to an extreme decision – to favor one of the two opposing experiences.

Sometimes the experience of spontaneous religiosity outweighs and shoves aside the feeling of absolute religious obligation and revelational subordination. As people in this situation try to free themselves of the burden of the revealed laws, their religious experience acquires a pure contemplative form – cognitive, moral, or aesthetic. In such a case, the practical purpose – to rectify man's actions on this earth and impose on him a tyrannical authority that will stand as a barricade in the face of attacks of boiling lust or evil instinctual cravings – slips out from under religious experience and practice. With the ebbing of the revelational, commanding element, which demands a particular lifestyle and appears in the guise of a religiously moral supervisor and overseer, the force of religion is annulled. Limiting the religious experience to its spiritual aspects leads to the elimination of its grandeur and influence. Under such conditions, religion becomes a leftover of culture. The force of religious decrees wanes, and personal anarchy begins to rise. It then seems to man that he himself is the author of the commandments, that he determines religion's purpose and goal. It seems to him that the formulation of the laws and their fulfillment are both subject to man's authority. He therefore takes upon himself the right to choose some laws and reject others. If he finds some laws to have a rationale from which he can benefit, he clings to them; if not, he jettisons them, as if everything revolves around free human creativity. The end result of this freedom is moral anarchy.

Someone who has attained knowledge of God only through personal inner awareness, and who does not feel the pincers of the revelational duress compelling him to adapt to the laws and statutes imposed on him by a separate supreme authority, is liable to disgrace himself in public. This is the tragedy of modern man: that, instead of subordinating himself to God, he tries to subordinate his God to his own everyday needs and the fulfillment of his gross lusts.

Religious commands (secular moral norms are insufficient) that break out with elemental force are the foundation of objective religious reality; those who deny them make religion a fraud. There is no need for apologetics, rooted in an inferiority complex, to defend the concept of the law in the Halakhah. All the statements by Saul of Tarsus [Paul] about the law as the cause of sin are nothing but *hevel u-re'ut ruah*, vanity and vexation of spirit (Eccl. 1:14). A rational philosophical religion devoid of revelational trials and commands is liable to publicly violate its own sanctities, under the influence of a secular social morality that has become defiled and corrupt. Religiosity lacking the objective-revelational element that obligates man to perform particular actions cannot conquer the beast in man. Subjective faith, lacking commands and laws, faith of the sort that Saul of Tarsus spoke about – even if it dresses itself up as the love of God and man – cannot stand fast if it contains no explicit commands to do good deeds, to fulfill specific commandments not always approved by rationality and culture. The terrible Holocaust of World War II proves this. All those who speak of love stood silent and did not protest. Many of them even took part in the extermination of millions of human beings.

C

Pragmatically, fearing God precedes loving Him. Western metaphysical religious philosophy, born out of the union of the Greek *eros* and the Christian *agape*, says much about the plenitude of love for the spiritual and the higher realms. But all its statements remain hollow utterances devoid of reality, because it has never understood fear in all its terrible essence. It therefore has often turned apostate and brought chaos to the world. From time to time, Satan has taken control over the realm of Western religiosity, and the forces of destruction have overcome the creative consciousness and defiled it. If not for Supreme Providence, peering out of the cracks of a mysterious, alien dominion, the universe would have returned to its primordial chaos. Only the experience of the revelation has saved the world from spiritual annihilation.

D

On the other hand, God wants man, as a natural creature with a natural consciousness, to worship Him. Man must worship his Creator not only out of the feeling of absolute decree and coercion, not only out of sadness and dread, but also out of spontaneous, variegated desire and aspiration, which gladdens the heart. The Torah commands us to serve God with joy (Ps. 100:2), with longing and yearning, out of enjoyment and happiness, unfettered pleasure and the soul's delight. When man does not see God and sense His presence at every turn; when he thinks of God only out of fear of punishment, with a cool intellect, without ecstasy, joy or, enthusiasm; when his actions lack soul, inwardness, and vitality, then his religious life is flawed. If man is not always aware of God, without any interruption whatsoever – if he does not walk with God in all his ways and paths, if he does not sense God's touch on his stooped shoulders and sweaty face in his hours of distress and loneliness, imparting a certain comfort and encouragement – then his service is incomplete.

When man becomes addicted to an ascetic existence, ignoring the necessity to improve and settle the world and to tend to physical and psychological needs in the real world, his religiosity is mediocre. God commanded man to take part in historical social processes and in the development of science and technology to benefit humanity. Anyone who withdraws from the real world is acting in opposition to the Creator's command, "Fill the earth and subdue it" (Gen. 1:28). The natural consciousness that was given to him by God is the source of man's longing for infinity and eternity. It is the wellspring of human feelings of joy and wonder, it gives rise to the stream of happiness and sweetness in life, and it impels man to participate in the process of actual creation; it tells man to progress, to elevate and improve himself. Halakhah, in accord with the natural consciousness, demands that man take part in the act of creation. In this way he fulfills the revelational command and introduces it into real life, thus raising this life to a wondrous sublimity. "He [God] did not create it [the world] to be chaos; He formed it to be lived in" (Is. 45:18).

As mentioned, man is divided in two. This was the primordial will of the Creator. Man needs both types of consciousness, both types of experience. If all of a person's consciousness and experience is natural, inner, rooted in his personality, then he is like a secular individual who stands outside the authority of religion. On the other hand, if he lacks natural consciousness and experience, and does not entwine them in his revelational experience within his comprehensive spiritual experience, then he is liable to abandon practical action and the real world. Unless there is a mutual relationship between the two types of consciousness and experience, the religious ideal cannot be realized.

E

Furthermore, the difference between revelational and intellectual experience is important for the issue of the exoteric and the esoteric in religion. Intellectual religious experience is an esoteric phenomenon limited to the few special individuals who live the mystery of being in all its beauty and sublimity. The masses, unaccustomed to deep inquiry and investigation, cannot taste the heady nectar of the religious experience that is born in the recesses of the spiritual personality and strives beyond the boundaries of the concrete. The universal riddle does not disturb the ignorant, nor does the experience of the sublime and the beautiful thrill the coarse-spirited. Scientific thought itself, despite all the virtues and achievements of modern democratic education, remains within the realm of the esoteric. The masses see nothing but its technological conquests. The essence of creation in all its purity is hidden from the many, and not for nothing did the Stoics weave the image of the *sophos*, or sage. The intellectual religious experience is therefore limited to the narrow realm of the lonely individual, the person of noble spirit.

Revelational faith proclaims its exoteric nature. It does not prefer the noble-spirited to the poor in spirit. The God who reveals Himself beyond the creation and outside the realm of cognition equates the great and the small, the philosopher and the obtuse one, the scientist and the ignoramus, the delicate and the insensitive. All of them stand awestruck by the Wondrous Presence, stunned by the apocalyptic vision, silently waiting to know what God will say. Distinctions in intellectual capacity or spiritual ability become irrelevant. God appears to His creatures in the majesty of His grandeur and imposes His rule over them, and who would dare pride himself before the Revealed Presence of *Deus Absconditus*, the hidden God? "That which a maidservant saw at the Red Sea [even] Ezekiel and the other prophets did not [see in their prophecies]" (*Mekhilta Beshalah* 3 [*Massekhet Shirah*]). The great goodness reserved for those who fear God is promised to every individual who performs His will. The revelation expropriates the right of religious aristocracy. All bow down before the majesty of God's grandeur.

F

These two directions, the esoteric and the exoteric, are very important for religious experience; it is impossible to do without either of them.

On the one hand, religion belongs to everyone. The whole community has a part in the world-to-come and in the faith that leads to eternal life. It is not one of man's luxuries, which he can choose either to accept or reject, but the source of his basic existence as a human being who leaves the realm of blind nature and enters the realm of living personal reality. Human experience is shaped by religion and acquires its primary establishment – eternal life. Undoubtedly, man's right to commune with Eternity and to acquire it is clearly not given only to the elite, but to the entire community. Everyone participates in the religious activity that redeems man. All Jews have a share in the world-to-come (*Mishnah Sanhedrin* 10:1). Many Torah portions address the people in the second-person plural. Everyone, without exception, is commanded to keep the commandments, and everyone takes part to the same degree in the holiness of the Jewish community.

On the other hand, religion must also provide the opportunity for individual spiritual ascent to the man who stands alone with his unique personality, with great sagacity and extensive knowledge, who looks out in great excitement from thrilling lofty cliffs into the divine expanses. The need for a unique experience of the divine, charged with spiritual depth and detached from the stereotypical experiences of the masses, exists as well – and perhaps especially – in the area of religiosity. Religion does not abrogate the individual offering, the soul filled with grace, radiant with the light of eternity and thirsting for God. It does not withhold a reward from creatures who are enfolded in their own essence and difference, approaching God out of individuality, aspiration, and originality of will. If the intellectual genius can derive the experience of eternity and infinity from the wonders of cosmic regularity; if the believing artist can derive it from the sublime and the beautiful; the just, God-fearing individual from the awareness of good and evil; and the mystic from the sense of God's hidden, obscure intimacy – and if, when they deepen and broaden their observation and contemplation of the Divinity and its achievements, their experiences become filled with a plenitude of inner grandeur, quiet joy, and sacred enthusiasm – may they be blessed. Religious perception is enriched by spiritual geniuses and great thinkers.

The cry of Korah and his followers, "For all the community are holy, all of them, and the Lord is in their midst, so why do you raise yourselves above the Lord's congregation?" (Num. 16:3), is partly true and partly false. Its premise is true, but its conclusion is false. It is correct that the external, exoteric holiness of the community of Israel, which obligates all of us to perform the commandments, does not distinguish between great and small. However, internal, esoteric holiness is dependent on the greatness, breadth, and depth of the individual. The greater the person, the greater his holiness. Many Torah portions address the people in the second-person singular. Inner experience is singular. One person's experience differs from that of his fellow, and the difference in the experience creates a difference in the holiness of individuals.

The fulfillment of Halakhah through the continuing activity of performing commandments is given to everyone – it is exoteric from beginning to end. Fulfilling the Halakhah through deep, comprehensive study of the Torah and through bold striving toward the crucible of the universe is given to the elite. In the latter realm, the Vilna Gaon cannot be compared with the Vilna shoemaker or water carrier. Individuals do raise themselves above [the rest of] the Lord's congregation. One lives with the community in the basic performance of the commandments, the basis of religious existence, yet he concurrently communes with his Creator under the rubric of focused action, in the enclosed realm of his lonely personality which separates itself from the community.

ಶ Chapter Eight
The Comforted Heart

A

Judaism says that the dichotomy between the quest for God and the revelation of God is only the surface layer of our awareness of Him. When we go deeper into the complexities of this awareness, we find an entirely different layer. Both approach and flight are raised in spiritual grandeur and ascend from the depths of nature to the heights of ontological and metaphysical conception. The utilitarian desire for reward and fear of punishment are transformed into love and awe, transcendent mysterious experiences. The antinomy of the attributes of justice and mercy appears in a new guise.

On the one hand, God is the Creator of the universe and the cause of all that exists. Man's primary knowledge is the recognition of the First Existent as that which keeps everything else in existence. Man must know that "the basic principle of all basic principles... is to know that there is a First Existent who brought every existing thing into being. All existing things, whether celestial, terrestrial or belonging to an intermediate class, exist only through His true existence" (Maimonides, Laws of the Foundations of the Torah 1:1).

True existence is the existence of God. Creation is the issuing forth of something from the bosom of the Infinite. The experience of a separate world that exists aside from God, by itself and in itself, is impossible.

Immediate ontological awareness concedes that there is no reality without God. The metaphysics of the book of redemption [the Book of Exodus] is expressed in the phrase "I am that I am" (Ex. 3:14). I necessarily exist, and wherever you find being, you will discern the illumination of My sole existence. Wherever someone or something "is" in the finite third person, the "I am" of the infinite "I" reveals itself. The "Let there be" of the six days of creation continues to exist because the "I am" of the fire in the bush reveals itself from within it. The Deity is the pure existent that brings everything into existence and encompasses everything. God's link to the world is not grasped only in the definition of cause and effect. It includes more than that; it is embodied in the continuous profusion of the bestowal of being. The relative creature is hewn out of the rock of the absolute. There is no existence without God, and there is no reality without reliance on Him. God therefore draws after Him the creature who yearns for complete existence, who senses the emptiness of his world and the dependence of his concrete being.

God is called *Elokei ha-Olam* – the world's God – as its Creator and Lord; but He is also *E-l Olam* – God of the world, meaning, the world bonds with God. The "it shall be" (*yihyeh*) submerges into the infinite "I shall be" (*Ehyeh*) which pervades the world bountifully. Man's aspiration in this situation is not eudaemonic; it is ontological. It is a bold aspiration to rise from nothingness to the God who bears and carries everything, includes everything, and grants being to everything. "Knowing Himself, He knows everything, for everything is attached to Him, in His being" (Maimonides, Laws of the Foundations of the Torah 2:10).

On the other hand, the God who conceals Himself under a protective canopy negates everything: [He is] beyond obscurity, separate, elevated and exalted, denying any open or hidden reality that claims the right of independent existence and turning into chaos those worlds that proudly declare, "We exist."

"Everything is as nothing for Him" (see *Zohar* I, 11b; *Tanya* I:13). God is the first-and-last, the one and the unique. His unity and His uniqueness abrogate any other existence, whether relative or absolute. God is alone, and there is no being other than His. Any link with God, whether as *Elokei ha-Olam* or as *E-l Olam*, is impossible in principle. The universe does not exist at all.

A separate universe that exists in contradistinction to God is based on a mysterious act of withdrawal (*tzimtzum*) of the true, one, and only Being, on the Creator distancing Himself from His creation. In the presence and infinite expansion of the Creator there is no place for a creature to exist, since the infinite swallows up and annihilates the finite. This is a mathematical equation, because Infinity + Finitude = Infinity, for what can be added to infinity? Man's aspiration to achieve complete being, which is fulfilled by coming as close as possible to the source of being, to the Infinite, leads man to eradicate his finite being by cleaving to the Infinite.

B

The creation's cleaving to the Creator involves the abrogation of the self as well as of the world's independence. It is a submerging of the finite in the infinite. The world exists when it folds up inside itself. It loses its existence when it breaks out of its circle [and moves] toward God. The fear of the annihilation of being is interwoven with the yearning for the elevation of being, a yearning that is fulfilled by coming closer to God. The spirit that longs for its divine lover wraps itself in the grandeur of His might. It turns, fades, and disappears into the terrible Infinity that fills everything and surrounds everything, that causes everything and outlasts everything.

"You shall set bounds for the people round about, saying, 'Beware of going up the mountain or touching the border of it'" (Ex. 19:12); "Let them not go inside and look at the sacred objects as they are being covered, lest they die" (Num. 4:20). The people of

Bet Shemesh peeked and died (1 Sam. 6:19). Man must not come too close to God. "You cannot see My face" (Ex. 33:20). Visions of God annihilate everything. "He is not to come at will into the Sanctuary… for I appear in the cloud" (Lev. 16:2). A priest who enters the *Heikhal*, the Sanctuary, is flogged, but if he enters the Holy of Holies he is punishable by death at the hands of God. He must not enter the place where the *Shekhinah* is located. One who utters the holy name of God in vain has transgressed a negative commandment. One who pronounces an unnecessary benediction has also transgressed a negative commandment. The Halakhah, in its sober, simple way, expresses a sublime metaphysical idea. Sometimes it is necessary for there to be a tension of great fear that is manifested in retreat. God constructs universes and destroys them, says the Midrash (*Gen. Rabbah* 3:7). The Tetragrammaton is both a noun and an adjective, and in its adjectival form it expresses two ideas: (1) the coming into being of what exists; (2) the annihilation of what exists.

The Kabbalah has revealed to us the secret of the breaking of the vessels and the story of the seven "kings" (from *Hesed*, lovingkindness, to *Malkhut*, kingdom) who ruled and "died" because they were unable "to tolerate the light that spread within them from sphere to sphere" (*Etz Hayyim* of R. Hayyim Vital, *Sha'ar ha-Kelalim*). Covering the lights streaming from the Infinite makes it possible for worlds to exist. The divine separateness protects being. The tension of love turns into the tension of awe and anxiety. Running toward Him is transformed into recoil from Him. Love stands up here to its fullest height and is freed from the instinctual longings of man, a living creature who is concerned about its reward. It takes the form of the eternal love of the creature for its Creator, of being for its source. Even the recoil is delivered from the straits of the instinctual fear of a hunted animal and becomes an expanse of spiritual awe filled with unrealizable longing and desire. This love is rooted not in man's instinctual but his ontological consciousness. The spirit fears God because it is impossible for it to exist in His presence. It loves God and runs after Him because it is impossible for it to exist without Him, outside of Him.[12]

C

These two approaches, the natural and the revelational, express a fully established truth. Judaism does not ignore psychosomatic man. His vital, natural, and eudaemonic yearnings and his instinctual fears are all very important for the development of spontaneous religious life. As mentioned, however, these yearnings and responses constitute only the surface layer of the experience of the divine, as a psychic experience born of natural vital responses and filled with the instinct for self-preservation. The link between God and man begins not in the pallid realm of the spirit, but in the fertile soil of the concrete individual. Judaism asserts that the spirit cannot soar if the living body with all its seething volcanic instincts does not move. The spirit cannot fly up to the heavens if the animal in man does not ascend with it. The spirit cannot become holy if physical man is sunk in the mud and is not drawn by the enchanted cords of the spirit to the wonderful circle of the yearning for God.

The longing and the fear together open a window to a supernatural realm. The experience of bodily and psychic longing and fear turns into an experience of sublime love and ideal awe. The eudaemonic longing is transformed into spiritual love, and the instinctual fear into spiritual awe. This love does not anticipate any reward, in contrast to the vital-natural longing, which is egoistic. The longing man serves God to obtain a reward; the lover and the idealist serve the Master without expectation of reward. This love is entirely directed toward a mysterious, metaphysical participation in the true, exalted existence. In order to achieve this purpose, it is willing to give up the pleasures of its concrete existence. It is an unconditional love. It rejects the small, narrow ego in order to cleave to the hidden infinite "I am" by virtue of whose existence everything else exists. This love includes an element of the act of self-sacrifice, akin to a burnt offering and incense, giving one's life to God in order to share in the essence of being. The reward, if we can speak of any sort of reward in this context, is the act of cleaving to God. This love divests itself of excitement as a necessary part of a blind emotional reaction born of natural instincts, and takes the form of free, conscious activity. Man longs for God out of the intellectual study of existence and penetration into the depths of the creation. Out of the conclusion that "everything is attached to Him, in His being" (Laws of the Foundation of the Torah 2:10), he yearns for his Source.

D

Awe is totally different from instinctual fear. Man as animal is haunted by dread and filled with opaque fears; man as speaking spirit (cf. Onkelos, Gen. 2:7) is filled with purposive awe. Fear is a powerful, vital response, dark and obscure, of bodily and psychic shock caused by an outside threat. It is an instinctual, emotional driving force that bursts forth at times of danger out of the mad desire to exist and assumes unrestricted dominion over man in times of crisis. Clear thinking has no part in it. It is imbued with the secret of the vital force rooted in every living thing, the desire to exist. Fleeing under the pressure of fear is instinctive, without any flash of enlightening will. Fear-driven man often runs away without knowing where, what, or why. Sometimes running away misses its mark, enmeshing the fearful person in the very danger he is trying to escape. Shouting "fire" in a crowded hall often causes insane running, with people being trampled as a result of the crush of the stampeding crowd. One who is afraid of death sometimes commits suicide in order to save himself from the claws of his fear.

To paraphrase a saying of our sages, fear is good in small doses; in large doses it is harmful (see *Gittin* 70a). A little is good because it manifests the normal vigilance of the life instinct. Too much is harmful because exaggerated or pointless fear leads to total insanity. Fear – as everyone knows – is the ultimate source of all neuroses and psychic anomalies in man. Not for naught did the Torah make use of the punishment of fear as the most terrible curse to seal the covenant in Deuteronomy:

> Yet even among those nations you shall find no peace, nor shall your foot find a place to rest. The Lord will give you there an anguished heart and eyes that pine and a despondent spirit... you shall be in terror, night and day, with no assurance of survival... because of what your heart shall dread and your eyes shall see (Deut. 28:65–67).[13]

Religiosity that remains too long in the realm of this terrible fear does not achieve its goal. It deteriorates into magic. The Torah commanded us to be in awe of God. Awe is born of the spirit that soars on high; its essence is an axiological position toward another, brought about by knowledge. Awe stems from assessment. Man assesses himself and "the Other." Out of this comparison and assessment he comes to feel awe, which begins with knowledge of inferiority and a sense of shame, and ends with spiritual recoil, whose essence is spiritual elevation.

Fear and love are mutually contradictory, but awe and love do not negate each other. On the contrary, they are entwined with each other. A great personality can bring about feelings of love and awe at the same time. When the storm of longing overpowers the lover and draws him to love, it also reveals the awe, which is a love fierce as death, that sometimes takes the form of silent suffering. I love the other and yearn for him because of his greatness and majesty, but this valuation itself also leads to the retreat of the lesser one in the face of the greater one. Coming closer leads to an axiological diminishing of one's self-image. Love contains equality of value but also the negation of value. "Honor your father and your mother" (Ex. 20:12) is juxtaposed with "Every person shall revere (*tira'u*) his mother and father" (Lev. 19:3) – honor and reverence go well together. The son does not fear his kind father and his gentle mother, and the Torah has never commanded us to fear our parents. Its emphasis is on reverence interwoven with enlightened, appropriate love. In this case, both of them [reverence and love] are rooted in gratitude. Similarly, our love and awe of God grow out of the experience of the connection between the universe and God. From this experiential awareness, the fiery attachment of love bursts forth, as well as the retreat of awe before His Majesty, a retreat which reflects absolute shame.[14]

৯ Chapter Nine

A

These two approaches express a whole truth that cannot be
faulted even in part. Man approaches God at a rapid pace,
where all his being, beset by the torment of fiery longing, is tensed
toward the encounter with his divine lover. He is swept away by
the surge of his yearning and carried aloft to the Infinite. Man's
being draws him with enchanted supernatural cords toward his
God, who is the source of being. But the unification does not occur. At the moment when only an infinitesimal step separates
him from his goal, and in a single instant he will embrace his
Creator, suddenly a repelling, deterrent force springs forth and
carries him in the opposite direction to unknown distances. He
runs toward God, but also recoils from Him. He runs toward
God, for how can man distance himself from God and live? He
retreats from God, for how can man attach himself to God and
live? Man's running toward and fleeing from his Creator, as he is
hurled back and forth by the two colossal forces of love and awe,
embodies the most magnificent worship of God. The Kabbalists
called this mysterious pendulum-like movement of the man of
God *ratzo va-shov*, "dashing back and forth." This movement was
revealed to Ezekiel when he saw divine visions: "And the creatures
were dashing back and forth like flashes of lightning" (Ezek. 1:14).
It is for this reason that the *Sefer Yetzirah*, the Book of Creation,

begins with the following description: "There are ten unsupported spheres which look like lightning and have no end, and His words dash back and forth within them; they run as a storm after Your utterance and bow down before Your throne."

B

The sages of the Halakhah expressed this struggle through two of the 613 commandments – love and awe. Love is the creature's cleaving to his Bulwark, "the yearning of the soul for the Creator, and turning to Him of its own accord so that it shall cleave to His supernal light" (*Duties of the Heart*, Gate of Love of God, 1). It is the creature's continually coming closer to the Rock of Ages, driven by longing and overcome by desire. Awe is the creature's recoil from the terrifying Almighty One, who reveals Himself out of infinity. Together they constitute the foundations of halakhic religious consciousness. Through them, man worships God with all his heart and all his soul. He who worships God roves back and forth between the two poles, which are as distant as possible from one another, with his whole being inundated with the struggle between love and awe. The man of God both loves God and stands in awe of Him. Halakhic Judaism affirms both the thesis and the antithesis and brings them together in a glorious religious dialectic, which gives rise to the vision of the Jewish people at the end of days. As Maimonides writes:

> This God, honored and revered, it is our duty to love and revere [*u-le-yir'ah oto*]; as it is said, "You shall love the Lord your God" (Deut. 6:5), and it is further said, "You shall revere [*tira*] the Lord your God" (Deut. 6:13). And what is the way to love and revere Him? When a person contemplates His great and wondrous works and creatures, and from them obtains a glimpse of His wisdom, which is incomparable and infinite, he will straightaway love Him, praise Him, glorify Him, and

long with an exceeding longing to know His great Name; even as David said, "My soul thirsts for God, for the living God" (Ps. 42:3). And when he ponders these matters, he will recoil frightened, and realize that he is a small creature, lowly and obscure, endowed with slight and slender intelligence, standing in the presence of Him who is perfect in knowledge (Laws of the Foundations of the Torah 2:1–2).

C

This strange dialectic is also reflected in the phrasing of the prescribed blessings, which begin in the second-person and end in the third-person [e.g., "Blessed art Thou, O Lord... such that everything was created by His word"]. The second-person expresses the aspiration of the community of Israel, intoxicated with love, to come closer to God to the point of tangency of entities, to the point of an intimate conversation within an I-Thou relationship. The beginning of the Jewish blessing is the mysterious striving toward God, which is always the cause of every motion, phrase, or discourse – the intense yearning of the soul for her lover. She desires her lover's presence and will not be satisfied with less than His full presence. As soon as this sublime soaring has begun, however, a terrible disappointment occurs. An unknown hand sinks the bubble of the "Thou" which appeared in the vision of the beloved longing for her lover. She is dragged along by her forelock to empty, silent, distant areas, spaces wrapped in totally obscure shadows of God; the second-person turns into the third-person, the Hidden One who peers out of the cracks, and a new note, imbued with the tragedy of bitter, silent despair, the note of concealment, arises from the phrasing of the blessing. The "He" appears. The intimate relationship is annulled, the link is dissolved, the friendship is over. The transcendent distance between the Infinite and the finite conquers all. We are speaking to the God who conceals Himself in His hidden tent.

D

The same dialectic is also reflected in the *Kedushah* (Sanctification) prayer, which begins with the prophecy of Isaiah in the Holy Temple of Jerusalem and ends with Ezekiel's visions. Isaiah saw God coming down from the clouds on high into the confines of the Temple in Jerusalem. He saw God when He revealed Himself out of his total, absolute separateness and when He came together with the universe and joined Himself to it, "And one would call to the other… 'His presence fills all the earth!'" (Isa. 6:3) – His indwelling permeates everything and fills the entire universe and joins together with it. Man is close to Him, and He is close to man. But Ezekiel, in exile on the Kebar River, encountered visions of God in the midst of a nightmare of historical existence, horror, and the pollution of life; he saw God very, very far away from the world, above the heads of the holy creatures and above an expanse which was spread out like an awe-inspiring sheet of ice. He heard a great roaring sound: "Blessed is the Presence of the Lord, from His place!" (Ezek. 3:12). God is blessed from His infinite "place," which rises above everything and is hidden from everything; God is blessed from infinity and eternity, from His perfect, absolute separateness. The framers of the *Kedushah* prayer added one question: "His servants ask one another, 'Where is the place of His honor, *mekom kevodo?*'" In other words, even though God is present in every place at every time and on every occasion, everyone asks where He is. For the Supreme One dwells in seclusion. The Jew observes God's coming closer to the world and, at the same time, separating Himself from it, and there is no distinguishing one from the other. At the very time that His glory fills the universe, the glory conceals itself in the shadows, and He is blessed from His place.

E

"You are my God, I shall seek You, my soul thirsts for You, my flesh yearns for You, in a wasteland, weary, without water" (Ps. 63:2); "My soul longs despairingly for the courts of the Lord, my heart and my flesh sing to the living God" (Ps. 84:3). So chants the man seeking the God who projects being and continuous existence, as if comforting humans for all their disappointments and hardships, and providing repose for the suffering, oppressed human soul.

"You hedge me before and behind; You lay Your hand upon me…. Where can I escape from Your spirit? Where can I flee from Your presence? If I ascend to heaven, You are there; if I descend to Sheol, You are there too. If I take wing with the dawn to come to rest on the western horizon, even there Your hand will be guiding me, Your right hand will be holding me fast" (Ps. 139:5, 7–10). Thus sobs the same person who just a moment before was singing a new song for God; now he flees the awesome God and knows that all his effort is in vain. God pursues him.

The love fierce as death joins with the great awe. The force drawing the person toward the wondrous supernatural joins with the force pushing the person back to the circumscribed system of nature; the cleaving of ecstatic desire permeates the withdrawal of awe, and an animating joy bursts forth from the silent agony of insignificance. The man of God, who is the man of the Halakhah, turns to and fro in his dialectic consciousness and discourse, caught fast in a thicket of opposites, without the possibility of escape or refuge. "The reward is in proportion to the suffering" (*Avot* 5:27); the worship of the heart is in accordance with the laceration of the heart.

∂❧ Chapter Ten

"This Is My God and I Will Imitate Him; the God of My Father, and I Will Exalt Him" (Ex. 15:2)

A

In the practical realm, this conflict is embodied in the principle of *imitatio Dei*. Halakhic Judaism placed this principle at the center of the universe. "And you shall walk in His ways" (Deut. 28:9) – as He is, so you shall be (see *Sotah* 14a). "This is my God and I will imitate Him" (Ex. 15:2) – as He is, so you shall be (see *Shabbat* 133b). Between the two poles of aspiration for full moral freedom – which bursts forth and rises up from man's yearning for God – and human subjugation and surrender to the divine decree, a decree that is imposed on man willy-nilly when he tries to escape from God, we find the desire to imitate God as a solution to the contradiction between moral freedom and subjugation.

The principle of *imitatio Dei* gives expression, on the one hand, to the terrible despair of the helpless man who is unable to realize his ideal – cleaving to God – which will grant him total and absolute freedom. A note of *tzidduk ha-din,* justification of the divine decree, is present in the idea of imitating God. Man surrenders himself to the blind, impervious fate that separates him from fulfilling his only hope of attaining his freedom by cleaving to God, saying, "Even though I cannot cleave to Him, perhaps I may be able to imitate Him." The act of imitation contains a confession of failure in his arrogant attempt to achieve total cleaving to God; if he were able to do so, there would be no need to imitate Him.

Yet, on the other hand, man makes use of the idea of *imitatio Dei* in order to allow a supernatural decree to be grasped as a free intellectual experience and dress it in the glory of spontaneous human freedom. In this situation, the unexplained revelational decree is blended with creative normative consciousness, turning into purpose-filled moral commandments. It seems to the man of God that the revelational command, which was imposed on him by coercion, was actually born in total freedom, out of the continual aspiration for ascent – from the darkness of natural opaque reality to the level of intelligible reality. If it is impossible for man to join with God and thus to become a partner in the act of creation, he can at least imitate Him by emulating His deeds, which symbolize total freedom. When man, animated by hope and yearning, moves toward his Creator in order to attach himself to Him, he gradually frees himself from the bonds of necessity and compulsion, and begins to dream of wondrous freedom, as if he were God's partner in legislating rules and formulating decrees and commandments.

His joy [over this freedom] is, however, only a temporary comfort. At that very moment, awe strikes the individual and pushes him back to the other pole. The unceasing awareness of eternal subjugation suddenly leaps up. Yet the person's joy is re-awakened. To relieve the burden of his moral subjugation, which is intertwined with the experience of awe, the individual compromises with his situation and is happy about the possibility of imitating his Creator instead of holding fast to Him. And then, once again the awareness of compulsion rises up. Through this dialectic of hope and disappointment, cleaving and departing, becoming closer and becoming more distant, the idea of *imitatio Dei* arises. It reconciles the two contradictory positions: divine decree with free individual creativity, the yoke of compulsion with spontaneity, reverence for the revelational command with the glorious vision of absolutely free will, the revelational experience and the experience of freedom.

B

As mentioned, *imitatio Dei* has elements of both absolute surrender and the exaltation of the free spirit. It has elements of the admission by the man of God that he has failed in some strange way, as well as his "crazy" insistence on believing that man has the power to come close to God and cleave to Him fully. Immediately after admitting his failure, the bankruptcy of his existence, he recants and denies his despairing utterances. In spite of the terrible chasm that separates him from his Creator, he imitates Him and follows in His ways. He adopts elements of the Creator's revelation for himself. New hope breaks out of the nooks and crannies of man's existence.

The names of God, in which (except for the singular name, the Tetragrammaton) the connection between the Creator and His world is revealed, obligate man to pursue particular ways of life.[15] The creature aspires to adopt those ways in which the link between the Creator and His creation is manifested, and thus to become similar to God. Halakhic ethics, which focus upon and encompass man's relationship to the other, whether a creature of brute nature or a human being, are enveloped by the Divinity's link to His world, and are realized by the imitation of this link. Maimonides expressed this idea as follows:

> We are bidden to walk in the middle paths which are the right and proper ways, as it is said, "You shall walk in His ways" (Deut. 28:9). In explanation of the text just quoted, the Sages taught, "Even as God is called gracious, so be you gracious; even as He is called merciful, so be you merciful; even as He is called holy, so be you holy" (see *Sotah* 14a). Thus too the prophets described the Almighty by all the various attributes "long-suffering and abounding in kindness, righteous and

upright, perfect, mighty and powerful," and so forth, to teach us that these qualities are good and right, and that a human being should cultivate them, and thus imitate God as far as he can (Maimonides, *Mishneh Torah*, Laws of Character Traits 1:5–6).[16]

This desire – emphasizing this idea yet again – is, in essence, the yearning of the bereft human being, branded with the mark of causal nature, to attain metaphysical and moral freedom and to deepen and broaden his existence by uniting with his Creator. But complete union is impossible, since man begins by coming closer but ends by recoiling. The man of God therefore makes do with imitation, which is intended to compensate, as I pointed out above, for the failure of his aspiration to join together. Imitating the deeds of his Creator and adopting His attributes constitute – to repeat the point once again – a tendency born out of love and awe together, out of running to and fro, out of the mysterious dialectic of the divine revelation of a God who is both honored and awesome. "And now, Israel, what does the Lord your God ask of you, if not to revere the Lord your God and walk in all His ways and love Him?" (Deut. 10:12). Walking in His ways is the central link in the chain of awe and love. Imitation is essentially both a revelational and a spontaneous phenomenon, directed at once toward total subordination and the achievement of liberation. Man comes closer to God but returns in frustration; he yearns for Him and also flees from Him; he both apprehends and accepts the revelational command. When he is in distress, he begins once more to seek God. The strange dialectical movement is reawakened; it returns to the original magical game of attraction and repulsion, approach and retreat. Out of this "game" arises the *imitatio Dei*: unceasing hope despite the clear knowledge of the disappointment that is sure to come. The imitation of God contains an intense effort to overcome the tragedy involved in these convulsions of the spirit. "And now, Israel, what does the Lord your God ask of you, if not to revere the Lord your God and walk in all His ways and love Him?" (Deut. 10:12).

৯ Chapter Eleven
From *Imitatio* to *Devekut*

I

mitation, however, cannot be enough. Although the vision of
imitatio Dei is distinguished by its glory and power, the road
that goes up to the house of God does not end there; it is still
possible for the individual to continue his ascent, from imitating – "And you shall walk in His ways" (Deut. 28:9) – to cleaving.
"If, then, you faithfully keep all this instruction that I command
you, to love the Lord your God, walk in all His ways, and cleave
to Him..." (Deut. 11:22). Imitating is linked to cleaving. From the
level of "walking in His ways," man ascends to the level of cleaving
unto Him. And here again the Halakhah appeared at the outset
and established two specific commandments – one of imitating
and the other of cleaving. Both are counted among the 613 commandments. Dialectical love – love that is cushioned with awe –
rises to the level of total, pure love. Intellectual yearning to cleave
to God appears hand-in-hand with recoil out of dread, in a sort of
running back and forth, turning into "madness" – the "madness"
of absolute love, ultimate and without successor. It is all clinging
and joining, all running toward without running away.

> What is the love of God that is befitting? It is to love the Eternal
> with a great and exceeding love, so strong that one's soul shall be

knit up with the love of God, and one is continually enraptured by it, like a love-sick individual, whose mind is at no time free from his passion for a particular woman, the thought of her filling his heart at all times (Maimonides, *Mishneh Torah*, Laws of Repentance 10:3).

Prophecy proclaimed that the eschatological mission of Judaism is the full realization of the singular name, venerated in the councils of the holy ones: "On that day the Lord will be One and His name will be One" (Zech. 14:9). The Aggadah, interwoven with Halakhah, followed suit, saying, "The world-to-come is not like this world. In this world God's name is written as Y-H-W-H but read as A-donai, the Lord, whereas in the world-to-come it is all one – it is written as Y-H-W-H and pronounced as Y-H-W-H" (*Pesahim* 50a). This world moves spasmodically from joining to separating, from the hope of coupling with the eternal, infinite Being to the fear of surrender to the absolute rule symbolized by the name A-donai. Outside the Holy Temple, the Tetragrammaton is not read as it is written. Only in the world-to-come will it be read in its completeness; the creature's aspiration to be joined with his Creator will be completely fulfilled, and man will cleave to his God without anything coming between them. "In the world-to-come there is no eating or drinking, no envy or competition, but the righteous sit with crowns on their heads and enjoy the splendor of the *Shekhinah*" (*Berakhot* 17a; Maimonides, Laws of Repentance 8:2). The One, the most hidden of all hidden entities, will be revealed in the light of His *Shekhinah* to the entire system of creation. The agitation of man's spirit, tossed between hope and disappointment, will subside, and the tranquility of eternal life will envelop everything. The divine dialectic is sealed in harmony, in the infinite peace symbolized by the Tetragrammaton.

The Kabbalists, who hear the weeping of the downcast *Shekhinah*, had this vision of the End of Days: "He said to the moon that it would regain its glorious halo" (prayer of *Kiddush Levanah*). The *sefirah* of *Malkhut* (kingship) – the *Shekhinah* that unites with the world – will rise to the heights of the *sefirah* of *Keter* (the crown). "For the sake of unifying the Holy One, Blessed Be He, and His *Shekhinah*, hidden and unknown, for the sake of all Israel," whisper the Kabbalists just before they perform a commandment. The agony and nightmare of the creation, its loneliness and desolation, are transferred to the bosom of the Infinite and are transformed, as it were, into the mysterious pains of the *Shekhinah*, as if God were sharing the separation of the creation and suffering the pain of its exile: "I am with them in their distress" (Ps. 91:15). The *Shekhinah* itself, as it were, is in need of redemption, and man prays for the redemption of the *Shekhinah*, with which he too will be redeemed.

B

Those who instituted the *Kedushah* [the communal prayer whose theme is sanctification] added a prayer to Ezekiel's prophecy [of "Blessed be the glory of the Lord from His place," Ezek. 3:12]: "From His place may He turn toward us with compassion," "From Your place, our King, may You appear and rule over us." When will You leave Your place, which is separated and removed from the creature you made, and gather us unto You? Jewish thought interpreted the foundational principle of divine providence as cleaving to God, as the desolate reality holding fast to the living, eternal Reality. Man must become an abode for the *Shekhinah* and strive to have God's eyes always upon him. The divine providence is correlated with man's coming closer to God. The sober, realistic Halakhah once again leads the camp but also brings up the rear, gathering up the fears of the religious consciousness, and coining firm concepts that reflect ways of actualizing the idea of cleaving to God. In the eyes of the Halakhah, this cleaving is not a vague hope sunk in some faraway eschatology, but a clear notion that can be grasped by a halakhic apprehension and whose fulfillment is rooted in the real present. The eschatological "tomorrow" is linked by the Halakhah with the simple, dismal "today."

The concept of holiness is rooted in the attachment between man and God within the framework of real life. According to the Halakhah, the holiness of certain places and times is identical with the influence of the *Shekhinah* in the here-and-now. The Land of Israel is holy because *Shekhinah* and prophecy are found there. When Jonah tried to escape from God, he left the Land of Israel. The holiness of Jerusalem and the Temple Mount are defined by the Halakhah through the presence of the *Shekhinah* in those places. Man who comes to the Holy Temple stands before God. In the Temple, the Tetragrammaton is pronounced as written. Fear subsides and love becomes stronger. The ten kinds of holiness with which the Land of Israel was sanctified are placed in the order of man's coming closer to God (*Mishnah Kelim* 1:6).

Time is sanctified if man, who has a temporal existence, joins with eternity, with God. Making an appearance in the Temple courtyard is the first of the commandments of the three pilgrimage holidays. And what is the essence of this commandment? Appearing before God, as it is written, "Three times a year all your males shall appear before the Lord your God" (Deut. 16:16). The holiday joy is revealed in man's joining with God, in standing before Him: "and you shall rejoice before the Lord your God seven days" (Lev. 23:40). When a quorum of ten Jews recite the sacred prayers, they bring the *Deus Absconditus*, the hidden God, whom the entire heavens cannot contain, into their confines. "And I will be sanctified among the children of Israel" (Lev. 22:32) – "in every group of ten the *Shekhinah* abides" (*Sanhedrin* 39a). When a group of ten Jews sit and study Torah together and complete their study, one of them stands up and proclaims aloud the vision of the *Shekhinah*'s redemption and man's cleaving to his Creator: "*Yitgaddel ve-yitkadesh* (May His name be magnified and sanctified)… in the world that will be unified in the future." But even when a single individual studies the Torah, the *Shekhinah* is with him, for whenever a Jew studies the Torah he brings about the gradual realization of the vision of the End of Days. The state of cleaving to God, whose essence is in the eschatological vision found in the prophecies of the End of Days, has begun to be realized even in this divided world, in the actual life of man with his flawed, sterile existence. Judaism has always known about the continuity between temporal and eternal existence, between the world that struggles to exist and the world that is redeemed, between the world that is polluted and the world that is all purity and goodness.

Chapter Twelve
The Heart That Cleaves to God

A

M ystical philosophers long for immersion in the silence of absolute unity. The Greek philosopher Plotinus and all those
who followed him were filled with such secret longings. But Judaism's goal is not the same as that of the mystics with their *via
negativa*, or negative way. The latter aspired to overcome the variety and uniqueness of man's personality, recommending the negation of people's variegated mental and physical existence for the
sake of attaining pure, simple unity with no objective content. In
denying the ontic independence of human beings, they came to
deny their essence as well. They therefore recommended the *via
purgativa* (method of elimination), which leads to *unio mystica*
(mystic unification). The individual must empty out the content
of his variegated life and freeze into a focal eternal point, lacking
all dimension and context, and confine himself to the One.

But Judaism, directed by the Halakhah, says, "This is not the
way." First of all, one cannot speak of man uniting with God, but
only of man cleaving to God. Second, man does not cleave to God
by denying his actual essence, but, on the contrary, by affirming
his own essence. The actual, multicolored human personality becomes closer to God when the individual lives his own variegated,

original life, filled with goals, initiative, and activity, without imagining some prideful, insolent independence. Then and only then does the personality begin to have a divine existence. Judaism insists that destroying man's uniqueness and originality does not bring man closer to God, as the mystics imagined. Man's road to God does not wind among faraway hidden places – in which man concentrates on a mysterious pyre in which his individuality goes up in flames – but, rather, among the spaces of real being, filled with movement and transformation. When the great question booms out, "Is it possible for man to cleave to God? Is it not written that God is 'a consuming fire'?,"[17] the mystics answer: It is entirely possible, for a fire will come from above and consume man's being as he is bound to the altar of his love for the Hidden One (cf. *Zohar* I, 50b–51a; *Ohev Yisrael, Parashat Shekalim*, s.v. *u-mah she-nitkasheh Mosheh*). But our sages of blessed memory gave an entirely different answer: One should cleave to Torah scholars and those who know God's name (*Sifrei* 49, to Deut. 11:22) – that is, one should live a life of value and elevation.

Because the mystics denied man's full selfhood, they made light of a way of life in which the religious aspect of the Supreme Primeval Will is fulfilled. They did not understand the ethical nature of religion. Inner ecstatic experiences are everything for the mystics, and all else pales into insignificance. Man's outward behavior and actions make no difference. Therefore they also disparaged the value of people's cleaving to one another in the social realm. For the mystics, social life is nothing but a waste of time. They exalted the state of seclusion. In their view, separating oneself from the community leads to introspection; this strips consciousness of its multitude of contents and shrinks it to a simple point, a point which is the link between God and man. In this way, they failed to grasp the place of living history in which is embodied culture, the product of man's spirit, since society both bears and is borne by the historical chain of events. Negating society thus entails negating the historical process.

B

The thesis of Judaism, as mentioned, is totally different. Our sages interpreted the commandment of "cleaving to Him" (Deut. 11:22) to mean cleaving to those who know Him. Cleaving to God is linked with cleaving to other people. The group with which man must form ties is an ideal society – the society of those who know God. This principle totally denies the mystics' assumption that ecstasy is possible only in a state of absolute withdrawal. On the contrary, Judaism states that God joins with the individual only in the merit of the community which is loyal to Him and seeks Him. If man separates himself from the community, he is not worthy of cleaving to God. The prayers exalting God's holiness may be not be uttered unless ten men are present – "And I will be sanctified among the children of Israel" (Lev. 22:32). Judaism has grasped the importance and influence of the environment; a select group raises man to a sublime height.

As emphasized above, Judaism here decreed that man cleaves to God through the full realization of his personality, by uncovering all the possibilities latent in the depths of his being. It is the broadening rather than the narrowing of the spirit that provides the opening to cleave to God metaphysically. In this sense, Judaism has given a measure of approval to the ethical view that fulfilling the ideal of coming close to God is the result of man's fulfilling his own essence through activities directed at both the self and the other. Contemplation without deeds and action does not redeem man. Fulfilling the revelational halakhic imperative is the most fundamental element in the fulfillment of man's religious mission; the Halakhah relates to both the individual and the community. One who is detached from society and the creative historical process loses his way in life. Man cannot exist either as an individual or as a social being if he does not link himself to the chain of historical events through which the character of the society is formed. The morality of the practical life, which is actualized within time, is on a higher level than abstract aspirations and experiences that are focused on eternity.

ৰ৺ Chapter Thirteen

"His Left Hand Was Under My Head, and His Right Arm Embraced Me" (Song 2:6, 8:3)

A

What is cleaving to God, in the Jewish view?

Judaism asserts that the source of terrible fear and fleeing from God lies only in the surface layers of religious consciousness. In the depths of this consciousness there is an experience of seeking that is interwoven with the revelational vision. There is a chain of development here, from the quest that ends in flight to the quest that is sealed by an encounter with the Creator. Out of the clash of finitude and infinitude, which begins with terror and horror, arises a strand of lovingkindness and compassion that draws man, bereft of salvation and thirsty for redemption, to God's bosom. At first, the yearning of love is joined with the repulsion of fear, but in the end a wave of pure love, ablaze with the fire of longing, surfaces and expels the anxiety and dread. The man of God begins with duality and ends with unity, starts with love mixed with terror and ends with love that transforms the repulsive power into attractive power and the deterrence into yearning. The individual who is fleeing suddenly senses the hand of the *Shekhinah* caressing him like a gentle, compassionate mother. He turns around, trembling and dumbstruck, covers himself with his cloak, and then uncovers a little of his face. He looks with amazed eyes, full of fear and astonishment, until his gaze encounters the smile of the *Shekhinah*, who is revealing Herself and running after him. Then the runaway who is being pursued immediately falls in love with his Pursuer, who loves him with an endless love. At the time of God's revelation in the bush, Moses hid his face, "for he was afraid to look at God" (Ex. 3:6); after the incident of the golden calf, however, he longed to see God's glory (Ex. 33:18), and he stood in the cleft of the rock (Ex. 33:22), laden with holy yearning, ready to cleave to his God. This is Judaism's longing and the wondrous climax of its world-view.

This experience embodies the idea that the desire behind the revelation is not that man be absolutely subservient or fearful, but rather that he be totally redeemed. The principal motive of the divine revelation is the infinite love of the Creator for His creatures and the desire for man's complete existence. The revelation is not an assault of the Eternal on temporal existence out of the wish to abrogate or abolish it. On the contrary, God cares about storm-tossed man – who plumbs the depths of reality in his search for God so as to uncover the total meaning of temporal existence and the possibilities latent within it, and emerges empty-handed (as was explained at the beginning of this essay). Fear is only the beginning of the journey for one who encounters God. The suddenness and surprise of the revelation fill him with terror. The incursion into time by the Eternal, into finitude by the Infinite, shake man's existence. At first, it seems to the individual that extinction lies in wait for him in the hidden mysteries of infinity and that extinction is about to catch up with him where he cannot escape it; his immediate reaction is therefore to recoil from God. The end of the journey for the creature man, however, is joy born of love, and permanent friendship between God and man.

Let us consider the way the Halakhah formulates the commandment of cleaving to God – *le-dovkah bo* (Deut. 11:22). As was emphasized above, the Halakhah says that one should cleave to those who know Him. In other words, those who know God cleave to Him; and man achieves his goal of cleaving to God by joining together with them. But then the question simply reappears: How do those who know Him cleave to Him? The simple answer is: Through their knowledge. It is clear that the Halakhah is not referring to abstract knowledge, which is of no importance. Study is an important principle when it leads to practice (see *Kiddushin* 40b, *Sifrei* Deut. 41). The pure life in the abstract, without taking on the form of the practical life, is not the aspiration of halakhic man or the man of God. When thought is transformed into will, and will turns into practical action that incorporates lovingkindness, justice, and rightcousness, then the thinking, desiring, and achieving individual arrives at the level of cleaving to God: "But let him that glories, glory in this, that he understands and knows Me, that I am the Lord who exercises lovingkindness, justice, and righteousness on the earth" (Jer. 9:23). The goal of knowledge is moral action, and so the term "those who know Him" includes more than what we see at first glance. "Those who know Him" are men of God, with achievement and aspiration, in whom study and practice, knowledge and will, are blended together in a unified spiritual entity.

In reality, this equation of knowledge, will, and action with one another is one of the principles of *imitatio Dei*. In Him, Blessed Be He, is revealed the absolute identity of intellect, will, and action. God's word is His thought, His will, and His action as well. By imitating this marvelous identity, man becomes like Him and also cleaves to Him. Once again: coming close to God begins by imitating Him and ends with cleaving to Him: "walking in all His ways and cleaving to Him" (Deut. 11:22).

B

This thesis still requires clarification, however. What is the epistemological and metaphysical foundation on which is based the possibility of cleaving to God in the sense of running toward Him without running away? The question remains: How is the goal of cleaving to God fulfilled in adapting to the unity of thought, will, and action? How does theoretical moral knowledge lead the creature to the Creator?

The secret of cleaving to God involves the principle of the identity of the knower and the known [i.e., in the act of knowing, the knower becomes one with the known]. This principle, which was raised to a wondrous height by Maimonides, who placed it at the very center of the Jewish world-view, sheds a bright light on man's attribute of cleaving to God.

This principle appears in two places in Maimonides' thought: in the *Mishneh Torah*, in reference to God's omniscience (Laws of the Foundations of the Torah 2:10), and in the *Guide of the Perplexed* (1:68) as an idealist assumption referring to human cognition – to finite knowledge at the time when cognition is operating.

The firm principle of the unity of the knower and the known in God's bosom – how does this work? To answer this question we quote the assertion of Maimonides in the Laws of the Foundations of the Torah:

> The Holy One, Blessed Be He, realizes His true being, and knows it as it is, not with a knowledge external to Himself, as is our knowledge. For our knowledge and ourselves are separate. But as for the Creator, Blessed Be He, He and His knowledge are One, in all aspects, from every point of view (2:10).

The division of realms between subject and object is [logically] prior to all intellectual activity. Every logical judgment expresses the link between the conceiver and the conceived. The knowing self faces the known "thing" and penetrates the realm of objectivity. When someone says, "This table is sturdy," he is asserting that there are two realms, that of the knower and that of the known. The table [the known] stands opposite him [the knower]. There is a confrontation in the act of knowing. The object [often] opposes the subject. Often it does not cooperate with the knower: on the contrary, it prevents him from knowing, and the object succeeds in its opposition. Sometimes the subject wins and penetrates the object's essence.

The confrontation between the subject and the object also occurs within the realm of the "I" [the self or ego]. In this situation, self-knowledge abolishes the unity of the personality. The separation between the perceiver and the perceived occurs to the unified consciousness itself. "Part of it [the consciousness]" takes the form of the subject, and "another part" the form of the object. A simple sentence such as "I exist" destroys the wholeness of the ego. Two "egos" appear in this utterance: The knowing ego stands outside the realm of the known ego. The ego that is the subject of the judgment claims that the ego that is the object of the judgment exists. In brief, all self-knowledge divides the personality into two realms – that of the subject and that of the object. Man cannot know himself unless he divides himself into "two" people – the knower and the known.

The division of the ego that comes into being through self-knowledge is multiplied to the extent that man continues to judge the self-knowing ego. For example, a judgment such as "I say that I exist" includes three aspects of the ego: (1) the ego as the pure judging subject, which transcends all judgments; (2) the "I" of the whole sentence, which plays a double role: as the subject of the whole sentence ("I say..."), and as object, in relation to the mysterious ego, the original knower, which makes the judgment and stands outside of it; and (3) the "I" which appears as the object of the "I" of the entire sentence, yet remains the subject of the inner sentence. This continuing plethora of strange figures, half subject and half object, is possible in self-knowledge, and proceeds infinitely. But the pure object that floats like a shadow at the beginning of the whole sentence will never disappear. Self-knowledge involves objectifying the known ego and separating it from the pure subjective ego. The ego faces itself and knows itself, like one who stands in front of a mirror and looks at his reflection as if it were someone else's. It thus turns out that self-knowledge means splitting the personality and alienating it from itself.

Obviously, for God, who is absolute Oneness, a split of the subject ego from the predicate ego is *a priori* inconceivable, for it would abolish, God forbid, His perfect unity. God's self-knowledge is not the self's contemplation of a self-otherness, but a knowledge that is unified in all the ways that the self can be unified; a complete, absolute identity of the knower, the known, and the knowledge reigns in His heavens. The epistemological tension between objectivity and subjectivity that rules in the area of cognition does not reign in His heavens. "Hence the conclusion that God is the One who knows, is known, and is the knowledge [of Himself] – all these being One" (Maimonides, ibid.).

C

Out of this sublime premise, a wondrous concept emerges. Even in looking at the world, the Creator's knowledge does not exist in the form of an ordinary logical judgment that consists of a correlation between a subject and an object, as though God knew the other as an independent entity totally separate from the knower. While the elimination of the subject-object dichotomy from God's self-knowledge is connected with the principle of God's unity, the eradication of this dichotomy between the realms of the subject and the object, the self and the other, from God's knowledge of the world is connected with the principle of God's uniqueness. As explained above, God is both the One and the Only, eliminating the existence of the other, since "everything" exists only in Him and through Him. Everything takes part in His being and depends on Him. The existence of objects is explained by their being rooted in God. Thus the opposition of subject and object is impossible in the context of God's knowledge of the world. It is impossible to separate the world from God because separation from one's source of being is ontological death. The object of God's knowledge is not within itself and is not marked by objectivity, which would distinguish it from the knowing subject. Therefore God's knowledge of the world is one with His knowledge of Himself. God knows things because He knows Himself, "for everything is attached to Him, in His being" (Maimonides, ibid.). He knows the world that appears in relative, dependent reality, rooted in God. This knowledge of God is folded into His absolute knowledge. He is aware of His truth, which includes everything.

Two super-logical elements emerge from this principle: (1) the absence of the duality of subject and object in the operation of God's cognition; (2) the absence of the cognition of the finite world as an "independent object."

D

In his *Guide of the Perplexed* (1:68), Maimonides expanded this principle, introducing it into the realm of man. He concludes that human cognition is an "emanation from God through the Active Intellect," and that every cognitive act is an infinitesimal participation in the Deity's infinite understanding. There is no such thing as finite knowledge, and man cannot know anything except through God's transfinite knowledge. Within God, the knower unites with the thing known, and even human cognition, limited and relative as it is, is rooted in this type of wondrous unity. Maimonides therefore established an idealist principle – that wherever there is knowledge (including human cognition), there is a unity of the subject and the object. When one grasps the intelligible essence of an entity, one penetrates it and unites with it. Instead of cognition as an act of imaging external objects which retain their stability and independent existence even after they are apprehended (as asserted by the ancient realism of images), there is an active, creative cognition; it penetrates the realm of the object, conquers its otherness, takes it captive, and conjoins with it. At first, before the intellect acts, there are two separate realms: the private realm of the potentially apprehending subject, and the realm of the "something" that is to be apprehended, the potential object. Afterwards, when the person overcomes the potentiality and becomes an active apprehender, the boundary between the subject and the object is blurred, and the two of them join together, through the act of cognition, into a complete unity with no distinction between the "I" and the "thing."

When the individual is involved in active cognition, the difference between the principle of cognitive unity [as applied to] God and [as applied to] man is manifested in the contrast between continuity and interruption. Divine cognition is infinitely continuous. There is no division of "at first" and "afterwards"; it contains both potentiality and actuality. God always acts and always apprehends, and the activity of His cognition has no beginning or end. Therefore, the unity of the cognizer and the cognized in His realm continues forever. If God were to stop thinking about the world, as it were, and averted His face from it, then everything would revert to chaos: "When You hide Your face they are terrified" (Ps. 104:29).[18] Existing means always being attached to God's continuous cognition.

In contrast to this continuity, human cognition starts and stops; the individual exercises it from time to time, but also leaves it. At times when he is not engaged in apprehending, he is only a potential apprehender, separated and distinct from the object to be grasped and by which he is confronted. When one is involved in cognition and the potentiality becomes intellectual knowledge, he ascends to the level of a true knower, conjoined with the Active Intellect, and achieves the unity of the knower and the known. But when he remains idle and descends to the level of potentiality, he doffs the precious jewel of the Active Intellect that is united with the known thing, and the dualism of subject and object emerges.

God owns the earth and everything in it, and He gave it to man: "The heavens belong to the Lord, but the earth He gave over to man" (Ps. 115:16). To which man? To the individual who apprehends the world and knows that it is absolutely God's possession. Through his cognition he blends with the universe. The apprehending individual possesses the world, in a relative sense, because he unites with it through his cognition.

ॐ Chapter Fourteen

A

In light of what has been said above, we see that cognition is a metaphysical act joining the conceiver and conceived. The cognizing human being grows as his cognition does; he grows with every object and every phenomenon that is captured by his intellectual endeavor. Man's being expands through the expansion of his knowledge. The personality of the knower extends in all the directions of his multidimensional cognition. Man cannot be satisfied by being alone, his own essence enfolded within his own existence. He desires the profusion of the world in order to escape the straits of the "I" – to unite with the objective world and wondrous faraway places bordering on infinity. Through the act of understanding, which eliminates the dualism of man and world, of "I" and "it," the mighty will expresses the human yearning to cleave to the Creator. When man unites with the world, he is also uniting with the Creator.

The act of creation is, in essence, an intellectual act of the Holy One, Blessed Be He, as God of the world. On the one hand, God knows the universe as existing in a separate way and as unique, as if His thought were directed at some ontic "externality." God's revealed knowledge constitutes the existence of the world. The lawfulness of nature is the uncovering of the Supernal Will from its closed-off infinity. On the other hand, as mentioned above, even if the world is "other," it still exists within God. He is the source of being, its essence and its purpose. The "all" is included within Him. God's knowledge of the world is the knowledge of His truth – His essence as the *makom* [place] of the world, as the first and last Existent who contains everything, encompassing and filling all creation. The "other" continues to exist because it is imbued with God's self-knowledge. Within this metaphysical, epistemological riddle is concentrated the whole theory of existence. God revealed to Moses the secret of "I am that I am" (Ex. 3:14). Wherever there is "being" in the third person – the "it" – the "I am" of the "first person" of God reveals itself; the "let there be" of the six days of creation continues to exist because the "I am" of the burning bush is unveiled from within it. The word of the Holy One, Blessed Be He, is also His thought and His will, in which and through which everything exists. The world is the "object" of God's knowledge, yet it is rooted in the subject. The known cleaves to the knower forever, without pause. The world depends on God for its existence.

B

On the one hand, the Holy One's knowledge of the world is identical with knowledge of His absolute true existence. On the other hand, one who apprehends the world identifies with the world and, through it, with the truth of His existence. At the same time, the world also constitutes the object or "thing" that is apprehended by the apprehending individual. It thus follows that man is united with the world, since the principle of the identification of the knower with the known also applies to the realm of limited, discontinuous human cognition. It thus emerges from this assumption that the world is the object of both God's knowledge and human knowledge – a remarkable conclusion! Put differently, by knowing the world the individual knows his Creator and cleaves to Him. This is Maimonides' ruling in Laws of the Foundations of the Torah (2:2):

And what is the way to love... Him [i.e., cleave to Him]? When a person contemplates His great and wondrous works and creatures, and from them sees His wisdom, which is incomparable and infinite, he will straightaway love Him, praise Him, glorify Him, and long with an exceeding longing to know His great Name; even as David said, "My soul thirsts for God, for the living God" (Ps. 42:3).

Instead of contemplative knowledge, whose essence is to receive impressions and be passive, to represent and mirror, we encounter the dynamic, stormy cognition of man conquering the world and conjoining with it. Man apprehends the world and becomes one with it. God knows the world as the truth of His own existence. Man and God are united in knowledge of the world.

But the second half of the divine equation, "Thought = Will = Action," demands its fulfillment in the life of man who aspires to cleave to God. Man must imitate his Creator not only regarding the identity of the knower with the known, but also in the identity of thought, will, and action. Without fulfilling this equation, man cannot succeed in cleaving to God. Cognition is identified with will and action; the knowledge possessed by the Holy One, Blessed Be He, is not passive or contemplative. Judaism rejects the passive tranquility of the Aristotelian dianoetic [i.e., intellectual] life, which is quiet, focused on itself, knowing what is to be known without creative action. Even the Torah individual who has reached the level of the contemplative life also merely imitates the knowledge of what is to be known by withdrawing into a corner of thought, a closed-off refuge of contemplative cognition. The eudaemonic moral ideal is expressed in the elimination of dynamic moral aspirations. In contrast, Judaism proclaims "And God said," which is linked with "Let there be!" (see Gen. 1). God's word is His thought, His will, and also His act. He is – at one and the same time – thought, plan, and fulfillment. Knowledge of the world as knowledge of the truth of [the existence of] the Holy One, Blessed Be He, is also knowledge of His active will. God apprehends, wills, and acts, and He commands man to become a creature who apprehends, wills, and acts, who imitates Him and cleaves to Him through the blending of thought, will, and action.

C

Let us review these ideas, for they are very important. God created the world as a separate object, but He did not grant it independent existence. The world exists because it is nurtured by some of the infinite being of God.

Pure cognition, without dynamic initiative or practical action, has no impact. "But let him that glories, glory in this, that he understands and knows Me, that I am the Lord who exercises lovingkindness, justice, and righteousness in the earth" (Jer. 9:23). Knowledge without action serves no purpose. The fundamental principle [at work here] is that cognition is intertwined with acts of kindness, justice, and righteousness, suffused by will, aspiration, and fulfillment. This is the idea with which Maimonides concluded his *Guide of the Perplexed* (III:54). Contemplation and morality, what is and what ought to be, are blended. True thought is also moral: thought = will. The moral will is the essence of cognition. Both of them are revealed in the continuing creative act. When the individual apprehends the world, he directs his cognition at a lofty moral goal and translates his cognition and volition into a mighty act; he unites himself with the world he has apprehended, and through the world he cleaves to the Holy One, Blessed Be He. For surely the world's existence is rooted in the thought of the Holy One, Blessed Be He, as the thought of absolute truth and infinite moral will, which is all action and creation.

D

Apprehension of the existence of the world within God and the vision of cleaving to Him are the aspirations of the man of God when he stands in prayer on *Rosh ha-Shanah* [during the *Musaf* prayer] and prays for the realization of the Kingdom of Heaven on earth. "And therefore we place our hope in You, O Lord our God, that we may see very soon the glory of Your might, to elim-inate idols from the earth… and His kingdom will rule over ev-erything." The people of Israel do not pray for the world to be an-nihilated, as the mystics do, but for it to be repaired; they do not plead for the elimination of God's handiwork, His creatures, but for broader knowledge and deeper understanding. They want to abolish the idols of ontological pride, which [cause people to] to hold on to their brazen independence and throw off from them-selves the yoke of the revealed moral command. The man of God petitions: "Let there be a good, pleasant world, full of the joy of the righteous, the merriment of the honest, and the glee of the devout when the evil kingdom passes out of the world." This evil is rooted in the arrogance of modern man, who feeds upon the conquests of culture: evil embedded with intellectual conceit that is satisfied with its finitude and temporality and is not directed at the source of reason. The Kingdom of Heaven is the kingdom of true cognition, when the light of knowledge will shine on the entire universe.

E

But how can this sublime vision be fulfilled?

As mentioned, fulfillment occurs through the action of a cog-nition fraught with will and action – in other words, by man's identification with the revelational Supernal Will as expressed in the Halakhah, which translates thought/will into will/action. The revelational halakhic law emanates from God's thought/vo-lition [through] His infinite understanding, the understanding of the truth of His own essence and the understanding of every-thing. Thus, when the halakhist adopts the thought of the Holy One, Blessed Be He, he identifies with the intellect and the pri-mordial will of the One and unites with Him. The same expression of the unity of the knower and the known applies not only to the knowledge of His primordial will – the "Let there be" of Genesis, which is ensconced in the sensible world and is manifested in its order and continuity – but also to the halakhic understanding of the revelational command. It joins finitude with infinity. And how characteristic it is that our sages distinguished two aspects of the fulfillment of the commandment to love God, whose purpose and essence is cleaving to Him: (1) contemplating the acts of creation; and (2) contemplating the word of God, which appears in its objective form as the various branches of the Halakhah. Indeed, contemplating the acts of creation, when not accompanied by subjugation to the divine halakhic moral law, does not lead to love of God, or to cleaving to God, or to the unification of the knower and the known.

ફ Chapter Fifteen

A

Judaism's aspiration to raise human consciousness to the level of spiritual consciousness, a level which combines the natural human aspiration for God with revelational faith, is manifested in three ways: (1) the rule of the intellect; (2) the elevation of the body; (3) the perpetuity of God's word.

What is the rule of the intellect? The special importance that the Halakhah bestows upon reason is so salient that it symbolizes the entire character of the halakhic approach. Intellect is the final arbiter in all matters of law and judgment. The content of the Halakhah, whose essence is revelational, is subjugated to the essence of rational cognition. Studying the Torah is a cognitive occupation like any other intellectual activity. The only authority is reason. The Halakhah expels from its realm all mysterious obscurity, whispers of intuition that are beyond rational cognition, and even supernatural revelations. A prophet who expresses his opinion on matters of Torah law in the form of a prophecy is punishable by death. The background [of the law] is revelational/ apocalyptic – both the written and the oral Torah, which were given to Moses at Sinai – but the swirl of colors painted upon it is "cognitive/natural." Human thought, which is subject to the principles of logic, has "dared" to penetrate into and occupy a realm that does not belong to it.

The freedom of inquiry and investigation in the field of the Halakhah is enormous. Torah scholars have to deduce new ideas from old ones, create new and original concepts and specific methods, and delineate distinct realms of thought. Deepening one's understanding and revealing innovative, enchanting horizons of knowledge – these are of the essence of the Halakhah. There is no change or reform within the Halakhah, but there is unlimited innovation (*hiddush*). When innovation is weakened, the Halakhah becomes sterile. Those who disparage us say that the Halakhah has become fossilized, God forbid, that it contains no creative activity. These people have never studied a page of the Talmud and have not partaken of the creativity and innovation in the Halakhah. They believe that Rabbenu Tam did not introduce any new ideas, nor did Maimonides, nor Nahmanides, nor the Gaon of Vilna, nor Rav Hayyim of Brisk. How ludicrous this accusation is! The aforementioned *rishonim* and *aharonim* [medieval and modern commentators] created new worlds that are breathtaking in their beauty and sublimity. They were among the greater innovators in halakhic thought. Anyone who is acquainted with the halakhic methodology, so epistemologically complex, that has been transmitted from one generation to the next by the *rishonim* and the greatest of *aharonim*, commentators on the Talmud, must admit that the sweep and scope of its ideal-deductive creative thought, its analytic acuity, its subtlety of abstraction and its systematic consistency are at least the equal of the other abstract and precise intellectual disciplines. Indeed, it is even superior to them. The principle of methodological unity and the coalescence of many free constructs into one conceptual whole – the most fundamental principle of any cognitive understanding – stands at the center of halakhic cognition.

Of course, the freedom of halakhic inquiry is bounded by a categorial restraint. The Halakhah cannot free itself from its subordination to a system of *a priori* postulates; it begins and ends with this system. Scholarly inquiry, however, is always connected with some system of postulates – it does not begin from a cognitive void. Freedom of cognitive creation means free cognition within a framework of ideal postulates. Transformations of form and content have taken place in recent years in our conception of physical and mathematical reality; and despite the fundamental changes in the epistemological interpretation of the set of axioms that classical theory of knowledge deemed a system of fixed, stable premises underpinning its theories, and which deductive science considers its "absolutely" secure basis, the fact of their [the axioms'] postulation remains. For example, scientific conceptions of space and time, of substance and causality, have been utterly transformed by the theory of relativity and quantum theory; scientific thought, however, has not yet freed itself of these postulates, which underpin the conception of the cosmic drama and leave their mark on the entire enterprise of objectifying the chaos of sensation. Although modern science has dared to attack the categorial system and adapt it to the needs of a "strange" facticity that it has not interpreted, it has not freed itself of having to postulate it. On the contrary, its ideal, *a priori* nature is emphasized all the more.

Deep investigation is not required to see that halakhic thought, rooted in a revelational foundation, cannot control its own postulates as does scientific thought. It has to accept them as they are. Nevertheless, halakhic thought, too, enjoys great, marvelous freedom. There is a combination here of two contrary elements: the revelational and the rational. The Halakhah is opposed to any change in the set of axioms; it is subordinated to tradition. Yet it seeks novel understanding, the veritable apple of its eye. In every generation man must deeply investigate the foundations of the Halakhah: the definitions of its concepts, its epistemic principles, and the ordering of its achievements. The goal of halakhic inquiry is to hew out new ideas and fresh, surprising conceptions. Studying the Torah means innovating and embellishing Torah thought. The framework of postulates is fixed, but within this very framework halakhic understanding penetrates into the depths, erupts and rises to the heavens. It has the freedom to inquire, build, and tear down, to grind mountains to dust with its fine distinctions, to make comparisons and deductions and create ideal concepts and design a new world. Even the postulates themselves, despite their stability, are filled with fresh, vital content. One cannot look at the world of the Halakhah without seeing perpetual motion and continuous flow. Studying the Torah is an act of free spiritual creation. [It involves] epistemological qualities and noetic values that live and are nourished by the creative spirit and mastery of the thinking individual, who thereby gains entry into the revelational sphere and makes it his own. Revelational consciousness is absorbed into cognitive consciousness with its innovational thinking. The Holy One, Blessed Be He, gave the Torah to Israel and commanded us to innovate and create.

B

What is the elevation of the body? It is [the basic teaching of] the entire Torah – everything else is interpretation. Judaism is aware of the strange dualism that splits man's experience and that general ethics wonders about: natural existence, which is dumb and unresponsive; and spiritual existence, which possesses thought and intention. But in contrast to general thought, which morally and metaphysically despairs of the natural element within man and devotes itself entirely to the spiritual and the rational, Judaism proclaims the redemption of the body: the deliverance of biological existence from the thick darkness of meaningless, undirected bestial drives.

Judaism is almost entirely involved in real bodily existence, in physiological functions. The subjects of the Halakhah are the parts of the human body. There are 248 positive commandments, corresponding to the 248 limbs of the body; the 365 negative commandments correspond to the 365 sinews. A medieval catalogue, known as the *Sefer Mitzvot Katan*, the "Small Book of the

Commandments," arranged the 613 commandments according to the body parts on which they depend. Halakhah aims to sanctify man's body, refine the bestial aspects of human life with all their lusts and drives, and raise them to the level of divine service. But this refining process does not take place in a crucible of denial and deprivation; [it occurs by] stamping the natural aspects of human existence with direction and purposefulness. Combining the beast in man with his divine image purifies and sanctifies the body. This union is accomplished by imposing the yoke of the halakhic commandments on the body. The purpose of the halakhic imperative is not to label man's sensual body as impure and thus reject it, but to purify it and draw it closer to God. The halakhic factor, when applied to pleasure-filled, self-satisfied fleshly existence, an existence driven by untamed instincts and made insensitive by savage lusts, bestows the glory of the *Shekhinah* on the human body.

The Halakhah enjoins man to take no less pleasure than the hedonist in the glory and splendor of the creation. The pleasure of halakhic man, however, is refined, measured, and purified – the enjoyment of one who has penetrated the furnace of lust and understood its nature. It contains something of the aesthetic attitude of the skeptic, who has tasted his fill of the world but not found satisfaction, as well as something of the moral discipline of the man of duty, who is afflicted by his drives but manages to overcome them. The Torah has never forbidden man the pleasures of this world, nor does it demand asceticism and self-torture. The Talmud expresses this idea as follows:

> R. Elazar Ha-Kappar says, [When the Torah says], "And he [the Nazirite] shall make expiation on his behalf for his sin against the spirit" (Num. 6:11), what spirit has he [the Nazirite] sinned against? It is because he caused himself suffering by refraining from wine. And we can make a deduction here from the lesser to the greater [evil]: If a person who has caused himself suffering only by refraining from wine is called a sinner, then

one who causes himself suffering by refraining from everything
is all the more so (*Nedarim* 10a).

A Jew makes a blessing on the real world; the entire cosmos requires blessings and praises.

Halakhah abhors the chaos in pleasure. A body enslaved to nature, seized with panic before the gathering of mighty forces of desire, falls upon pleasure and wrings every last drop out of it. The Halakhah enjoins man from the hysteria of desire and madness. The sort of pleasure that the Halakhah recommends avoids excessive intensity, stimulation of the nerves, and intoxication of the senses. Instead, it has the beauty of the refinement and splendor of life's aesthetic elements. When man takes pleasure in the world in accordance with the view of the Halakhah, his pleasure is modest and delicate, an enjoyment which avoids the mania of sexual desire and the frenzy of gluttony.

The animalistic behavior of eating, upon which man's life depends, has been refined by the Halakhah and transformed into a religious ritual and an elevated moral act. "You shall eat, in the presence of the Lord your God, in the place where He will choose to establish His name, the tithes of your new grain and wine and oil, and the firstlings of your herds and flocks, so that you may learn to revere the Lord your God forever" (Deut. 14:23). A commandment of this sort cannot be understood by Greek moral philosophy. The beast eats; man thinks and cognizes the spiritual, the general, and the ideal. The intellect comes close to God, but the stomach does not. "You shall eat in the presence of the Lord" – can there be two more extreme opposites than these? But it is nevertheless so! The Halakhah gave priority to eating in the presence of God over prayer. Eating portions of sacrificed animals, eating the paschal lamb, eating the second tithe and other offerings of lesser sanctity, eating matzah on Pesah, eating of the special sacrifices on the three pilgrimage festivals – all these are positive commandments that are counted among the 613 commandments according to all opinions, whereas prayer is among the 613 only as counted in Maimonides' system. The joy of the festivals depends on eating sacrificial meat when the Temple exists, and outside the Temple – or when it no longer exists – eating ordinary meat and drinking wine. This joy is the joy of man in the presence of his Creator. The purpose of eating the sacrifices is the enhancement of one's awe of God: "You shall eat… so that you may learn to revere the Lord your God forever" (Deut. 14:23). Joy is maintained through eating. Only in the case of one verse do we say that joy is embodied in another action – [the verse pertaining to] holding the *lulav*. This verse occurs among the laws of the festivals in Leviticus: "…and you shall rejoice before the Lord your God seven days" (Lev. 23:40). Here too there is a concrete action – lifting the *lulav*.[19]

The act of eating does not represent some mysterious symbolic form of worship; it is merely the ordinary eating that man enjoys and with which he satisfies his hunger. On the contrary, if one eats when he is not hungry, so that he is disgusted by the act of eating, it is doubtful whether he has fulfilled the associated commandment. The Halakhah obligates man to eat matzah with appetite, to eat the sacrificial meat roasted in the manner of royalty. An animal function can be raised to the level of original, perfected divine worship. Wine, the symbol of licentiousness and drunkenness, of the frenzied worship of Bacchus, is transformed into the cup over which blessings are recited and the libations for the altar upon which man chants songs of praise for his Creator – there is even a rule that one does not chant songs of praise for God except with wine (*Berakhot* 35a) – and sanctifies everything in the world with a divine holiness.

When someone eats sacrificial meat, he also feeds strangers, orphans, and widows. Such eating constitutes [not only] religious worship, but also an act of social morality: including needy people in the circle of one's enjoyment. Friendship and love are embodied in physiological functions through which flesh-and-blood human beings demonstrate their belonging to a society and their connectedness with others.

Socratic Greek thought attempted to give the dinner table

the character of an intellectual gathering devoted to philosophical discussion, in which men of ideas participated. This is the true essence of the Greek symposium. Judaism refused to do this [i.e., to convene such a gathering]. It devoted the dinner table not to human intellectual matters, but to divine intellectual matters, to discussions of the Torah that we received from God. Every meal must be devoted to discussions of the Torah. Our sages said, "If three people eat at the same table and do not discuss the Torah, it is as if they have eaten from sacrifices to the dead [i.e., idols]" (*Avot* 3:3). Judaism's aspiration is not intellectual but moral – revelational. The purpose of all cognitive activities is the fulfillment of the holiness of the body and the spirit. Eating is an act that realizes the idea of holiness, whose meaning is the sanctification of both body and soul. If man eats properly, in accordance with the requirements of the Halakhah, then he is eating before God, serving Him with this "despised" function, and cleaving to Him. A group of Jews who have eaten together summon one another formally to recite blessings after the meal. The individuals who are eating are joined into a spiritual bloc, which is elevated to the status of a group among whom God dwells.

The halakhic concept of fasting is not intended to be ascetic. Instead, it is a temporary withdrawal from the daily trivialities and vanities of this world and the petty issues of the battle for survival, so as to devote oneself to moral accounting and acts of repentance. Although there is no obligation of enjoyment on Yom Kippur, there is a duty to honor the day; the Midrash (*Lev. Rabbah* 34:15) states that the verse "To honor the sanctified of the Lord" (Isa. 58:13) refers to Yom Kippur. It is considered a holiday and abolishes the seven-day and thirty-day mourning periods. Thus, there is a note of joy even in this day of fasting. Nor is the status of the Nazirite expressed in an aspiration for asceticism. The telos of Naziritehood is to sanctify bodily existence, not to avoid it. On the contrary, the Nazirite is forbidden to become ritually impure through contact with the dead; man, whose entire body is holy, must not be a witness to the degeneration of life.

C

Neither Greek philosophy nor Christianity grasped the moral and metaphysical aspects of sexual intercourse. Only the Halakhah gives this act a solid basis in religious life; the commandment to "be fruitful and multiply" (Gen. 1:28) is the first one in the Torah. Marital life is pure and blessed. The life of a bachelor, even if he has never sinned, runs contrary to the view of the Halakhah. One who is not married has no joy, no blessing, and no Torah (*Yevumot* 62b). The Holy One, Blessed Be He, Himself engages in match-making (*Gen. Rabbah* 68:3–4). The joy of the bride and groom is very important, and anyone who participates in it receives a great reward (*Berakhot* 6b). A husband is required to have relations with his wife at regular intervals, according to his physical ability and the conditions of his work (*Mishneh Torah*, Laws of Marriage 14:1; see *Ketubbot* 61b–62a). The Halakhah's laws of sexual intercourse, which are based on psychological principles and sexual hygiene, are marvelous for their clear-headedness and "modernity." How much concern, along with delicate and intimate understanding, is found in these laws! The same iron-clad Halakhah that forbids sexual intercourse when the wife is menstruating and establishes preventive measures around this restriction, also imposes an absolute duty upon man to have intercourse with his wife periodically out of love and affection. The Halakhah established the concept of "intercourse which fulfills a commandment."

Man worships his Creator with his body, his eating, and his sexual activity, and this worship is preferable to worship through prayer.[20] Look and see how much is written in the Torah and the Talmud about the laws of forbidden sexual relations and forbidden foods, and how little is written about the laws of prayer. Many people who gorge themselves on food like a predatory animal in its lair and defile their sexual love life are able to pray to God on bent knee, but not many can eat in the presence of God and sanctify themselves while under attack by the sexual drive. Wherever there is a possibility of sexual activity, the Torah enjoins sanctity.

Maimonides calls his compilation of the laws of forbidden sexual relations and forbidden foods by the name "The Book of Holiness." Sexual relations reflect the image of the human being as differentiating himself from the beasts and (while still in his body) soaring to the heights. Socratic/Platonic metaphysics, which has had such a great influence on Christianity, insists that the spirit rises upward while the body goes downward, that man is crowned with a garland of reason and has the power to soar up to the world of the *Logos* by devoting himself to a spiritual and intellectual calling that does not involve his real animal existence. Judaism declares [in contrast] that man earns eternal life by transforming his purposeless, animalistic, temporal existence into the holy life of the man of God. The former speaks about the continuing existence of the general [collective] soul, while the latter insists on individual immortality and the reawakening of the dead. The body will emerge from its grave in all its glory.

Physiological drives are sanctified through the moral commandments, which are not intended to subdue this world, but rather to place upon it the crown of royalty. The Halakhah allows the creature of nature to break through to pellucid radiant expanses and new skies. It is not only the spirit but also the beast in man that worships the Creator. The *Shekhinah* hovers over the abyss of lust and man's animalistic, instinctual essence, and sanctifies them. There are established regulations for using the toilet. Even there (and perhaps especially there) man must sanctify himself in the presence of his Creator. "Further, there shall be an area for you outside the camp, where you may relieve yourself. With your gear you shall have a spike, and when you have squatted you shall dig a hole with it and cover up your excrement. Since the Lord your God moves about in your camp… let your camp be holy" (Deut. 23:13–15).

Man worships God even when he is sitting on the toilet, and therefore he must know how to sit and how to wipe himself. R. Akiva followed R. Joshua into the outhouse and learned three things from him (*Berakhot* 62a). This too is part of the Torah, and he needed to learn it. When Jewish religious liberalism complains about the traditional Halakhah, saying, "What sort of a religion is this – a religion of the stomach?" it is saying something of substance without realizing it. Yes, indeed, the Halakhah is a doctrine of the body; but there lies its greatness. By sanctifying the body it creates one whole unit of psychosomatic man who worships God with his spirit and his body and elevates the beast [in him] to the eternal heavens.

⋟ Chapter Sixteen

A

When Judaism placed the rule of reason and the sanctification of the body at the center of its world, it eliminated the dualism that encases man's consciousness of God. When the revelational content is directed at real, natural existence, with all its colors and tones, the abyss in religious experience is closed up. The halakhic ideal is embodied in its striving for joint revelational and intellectual activity. Halakhic man grasps supra-rational topics and discusses them in an objective, rational manner. The world of spiritual values was created according to a vision of a supra-ontological, revelational world. The thread of eternity winds through the achievements of the intellect and joins it to become a perfect whole. Revelational faith does not clash with what exists or deny its importance. On the contrary, its teaching is a reality-based doctrine, a doctrine of what exists, whose purpose is the sanctification of biological existence, and whose strategies are inherent in logical thought. This is a strange phenomenon: on the one hand the Torah embodies a supra-cognitive, supra-ontological revelational vision, yet on the other hand it is grasped by the human mind and constricts itself into the ontological realm. Wherever its alien character is found, its glory is found as well. Transcendence descends into limited, contingent being; the reality outside the limits of human understanding is absorbed by a reality that is accessible to human understanding. The Divinity emanates hidden glory into a world interpreted by the human mind in its entire spectrum of colors.

B

The objective Halakhah is enclosed within the realm of the actual. Its object is the world that encompasses us completely. It approaches this world with a normative yardstick. Yet, in order to formulate the norm in halakhic terms, objective Halakhah requires a clear acquaintance with the object. Without such knowledge, it is totally impossible to discuss the world from a halakhic standpoint. There is therefore an intimate connection between the objective, normative Halakhah and the scientific cognition of the free, creative intellect.

There is no scientific or technological innovation that is not of interest to the Halakhah. Efforts are made in the halakhic consciousness to penetrate the secrets of the scientific world. For example, the laws of *kil'ayim* (forbidden hybridization) directly require a knowledge of the morphology of plants and animals; the laws of offerings to the priest, of tithes, of forbidden fruit of the first three years, and of first fruits, all of which depend on the measurement of the growth of plants, require a knowledge of organic chemistry. The laws of Sabbath boundaries [demarcating private and public domains], of [what constitutes a valid] *sukkah*, of *kil'ayim*, and of the enclosure within which a corpse imparts impurity – all involve not only arithmetical techniques, but also a mathematical and conceptual grasp of space. What constitutes forbidden carrying of objects from one domain to another on the Sabbath and the actions of lifting up an object or putting it down; direct and indirect causation in murder, injury, or damage; the forbidden displacement of certain objects (viz., *muktzeh* objects) on the Sabbath; less direct and more direct forms of causation – all involve understanding the principle of causality in general and the laws of mechanics in particular. What constitutes purposeful action [on the Sabbath or festival]; offhand [and therefore exculpable] violations of the Sabbath or festival; actions that are performed by mistake or with malicious intent; compulsion; the intent of seller and buyer in a transaction – all involve the psychological and epistemological concept of intentional acts and the moral and metaphysical idea of free will. The times of day (sunset, sunrise, nightfall, dawn, twilight) are based on astronomical calculations as well as on the laws of optics. The visual signs of skin diseases and blood emissions involve both the physical and the psychological theories of color. The laws of menstrual impurity and seminal issue, the determination of a menstrual pattern, the blood of a woman's initial intercourse, and the signs of a fatal disease – all directly involve a knowledge of the anatomy, physiology, and pathology of the human body.

The Halakhah deals with the laws of government and political administration, sociological issues such as state, society, family life, and the interaction between individuals, marital status and similar matters. The laws of *miggo* [by which a person's statement is believed because if he were lying, he would have put forth a still more advantageous statement], of *umdana* [estimation of intent], of judicial discretion, of someone's being presumed to be a liar, of someone's being suspected of committing a transgression, of the nature of the marital relationship, and of levels of competence – all are determined by psychological and psychiatric concepts. The Halakhah involves itself with technological achievements in order to clarify its position on them. Electricity, airplanes, refrigerators, microphones, telephones, and the like are topics for halakhic discussion. To define the laws, the Halakhah must understand the scientific background and structure of these things. Galileo said that nature is written in [the language of] mathematical equations. It is no overstatement to say that Halakhah writes in the language of orderly scientific reality.

ಾ Chapter Seventeen
The Prophesying Heart

A

*H*ow has prophecy been perpetuated?

The blending of revelation and reality is also found in the concept of prophecy. What is this concept? The beginning of prophecy, which is one of the basic articles of faith, occurs when God reveals Himself to man and directs His words at him. The prophet is taken out of the actual world into a wondrous, supra-rational, supra-ontological world. There he is commanded to return to the actual world, to repair it and purify it. The revelation in prophecy is God revealing Himself to human beings, not in order to take them out of this world, but to reform and elevate it.

In Maimonides' view, it is very important for human beings to seek God and prepare themselves morally for an encounter with Him. Although God does indeed cause man to prophesy and relates to him, he must search for God and prepare himself to encounter Him. God reveals Himself to man in times of crisis and distress even when the individual is not seeking Him; nevertheless, God still expects man to seek Him. Despite the supra-rational and supernatural character of prophecy, it demands that man be ready and expectant. One must prepare oneself for the revelation of the *Shekhinah*. This preparation focuses on penetrating "the secrets of the world" (*Hagigah* 13a), living a pure and holy life, perfecting one's halakhic ethical personality, and rising to the peak of cleaving to God. Here are the words of Maimonides about the personality of the individual who prepares himself for prophecy:

> Prophecy rests only upon a wise man who is distinguished by great wisdom and strong moral character, whose passions never overcome him in any matter whatsoever, but who by his rational faculty always has his passions under control and possesses a broad and sedate mind. When one abundantly endowed with these qualities and physically sound enters *Pardes* and continuously dwells upon these great and abstruse themes – having the right mind capable of comprehending and grasping them; sanctifying himself, withdrawing from the ways of the ordinary run of men… keeping his mind disengaged, concentrated on higher things as though bound beneath the Celestial Throne so as to comprehend the pure and holy forms and comprehending the wisdom of God as displayed in His creatures, from the first form to the very center of the earth, learning thence to realize His greatness – on such a man the Holy Spirit will promptly descend (Laws of the Foundations of the Torah 7:1).

Man must purify and sanctify himself through an effort of the mind and the will, and through creative acts producing mighty effects, so as to be prepared to hear the word of God. There is one commandment that includes all 613, namely, "You shall be holy" (Lev. 19:2), which in its essence is the commandment of preparing oneself for prophecy. The wondrous peak of the prophetic vision is man's moral aim. A personality worthy of prophecy is a supreme personality emitting light out of the darkness of a clouded world.

Let me recapitulate. As a phenomenon, the revelation of the *Shekhinah* sometimes precedes the person's preparation and perfection; indeed, God relates to man at a time when the glory of life is at a low ebb and ugliness has overwhelmed it. But [despite this], man must make an effort to reach the level of the revelation of the *Shekhinah*. Seeking such a revelation through knowledge and natural will [generally] precedes the supernatural revelation of the *Shekhinah*. Not only is the fact of prophecy – God's encounter with man – an obscure riddle, but even the quest for it, the search for eternity through temporality, is incomprehensible. Earlier we saw that the mind's demands link it to reality. But what sort of demands are they? We might say that they are demands for a cognitively framed solution to the problem of the mystery inherent in tangible reality. The mind demands of reality a logical formulation needed by the intellect, a formulation that will serve as an expression of eternity and link the message of the supernatural with the natural. The supernatural, in the Jewish view, is not separate from the world and is not hidden in some absolute confinement. On the contrary, says Judaism, there is a continuous transition from the concrete to the absolute, from the finite to the infinite. Infinity overlaps with our world and is combined with it into a homogeneous reality. What we call the supra-rational defines the limits of human understanding, but does not represent a total metaphysical separation from the real world. Yes, Judaism has firmly established that there is no terrible abyss separating this finite, limited world from the world that is completely good, absolute, and unlimited. Judaism links the real world with the super-worldly.

B

The commandment of preparation for prophecy, which is an obligation in Judaism, implies that natural consciousness and revelational consciousness belong to two different realms, and that there is no immediate continuity between them. But this is true only when [there is no preparation and] man encounters God against his will. Then the sudden revelation is mysterious and man recoils from it. However, when man encounters God after seeking Him, after praying and hoping for the revelation, then reason unites with faith, the free creative consciousness unites with the "compelled" revelational consciousness, and a relationship of question and answer, of longing and fulfillment, bursts forth.

Judaism says to one [who is given an unexpected revelation], "You have felt a great fear, you retreated when God appeared to you because you did not expect Him and you did not pray for Him to come, and so His coming terrified you. But this fear, which stems from your lack of anticipation and the suddenness of the revelation, does not occur with a revelation that you are hoping for with all your heart and soul. If you seek God and He answers your prayer and appears to you, then you will not be afraid of Him. You will be happy with Him, and you will find rest and repose in His bosom."

Obviously the search and the finding, the quest and the revelation, belong to different, incommensurable, incomparable realms; Judaism is not saying that the vision of the revelation can be brought about by mental effort. Such rationalism, which emerges from time to time in philosophical religious thought, lowers prophecy to the level of a pedagogical tool and distorts the nature of the divine vision. The revelation of the *Shekhinah*, in our view, occurs in a realm that is closed to the intellect. Yet God attends to man who seeks Him and longs for the revelational encounter. The revelation contains a sort of an echo of a response to the call of the one who seeks God, a sympathetic link of some kind with his suffering and torment. This response is formulated in a strange language that the mind is not comfortable with because it is impossible to adapt the essence of the vision to rational necessity. But God is pleased with the mind's quest as it strives for Him, and He pays heed to it. Considering prophecy to be a duty implies that man must hope for God to respond from the realm of eternity to man's question that bursts forth from the realm of the given reality.[21]

In sum, man tries to understand the wonders of the creation, the Hidden Intellect, and the Supernal Will of Mount Sinai reveals itself to him. At first it seems to him that the response does not fit the question. Man wants to understand the real world, and he is given knowledge of a revelational, supramundane command. He prays for intellectual enlightenment and encounters a decline of the rational and a clouding of consciousness, as if God were laughing at him. So man flees from God. However, as his knowledge is deepened and strengthened, the unity of the wonders of the creation and the command from Sinai begins to gleam until it shines and illuminates man's entire being. To the extent that the unity of creation and Sinai becomes clearer to him, man overcomes the split in his mind between rationality and revelation and stamps them with unification and oneness.

The only difference between creation and Sinai is the change of direction: from question to answer. The former is clothed in mystery, while the latter heralds the solution. Intellectual cognition directed at the creation is divided: half of it is logical thought, while the other half is the consciousness of the wonder of reality. Modern man's entire cultural outlook is full of contradictions and oppositions. It encounters nonrational elements that cannot be grasped by the mind. Physico-mathematical science encounters the living, qualitative reality; metaphysics encounters the blind and impenetrable substance, mechanical nature; morality encounters sin and evil; art encounters the ugly and the repulsive, and so on. The weight of the irrationality and inconsistency in the perceived world lies heavily on the cultural *Weltanschauung* (worldview). In spite of man's many human technological achievements and his conquest, to an extent, of matter, the eternal riddle continues to emerge from all the realms of the creation, especially those illuminated by reason. The words of the solution come from Mount Sinai: the God who is sought on the paths of the creation experience reveals Himself in the Sinaitic vision. The mind seeks and prophecy responds. The content of revelation is faith, bearer of the absolute imperative. The child of the creation finds his purpose and his path to perfection in the revelational consciousness, the ontological law – in the prophetic statutes.

If man hopes for a vision out of his good will, he bestows some of the glory of freedom on the revelation experience. The revelation does not cause recoil and flight. The man of God tries to hold on to the divine law and place it within his own realm. His intense effort is directed at mastering the revelational content and melding it with his ontological consciousness into a fresh experience drenched with light and favor.

The total compulsion that enwraps man reveals itself to be a savior, a redeemer who has come to provide him with his personal uniqueness and independence. He is bound to the authority of the Most High, but he is happy with this lot, since his subordination to the Divinity frees him from the chains of the natural world and raises him to the level of freedom of the man of God. The revelational law is transformed into an "existential" law, which is received by the mind and blends with it in its bold, free flight. The individual, who began with a search for a reality pregnant with freedom, encounters the compulsion of the Numinous One and ends with the experience of freedom. "There is no one as free as one who is engaged in the study of the Torah" (*Avot* 6:2). The heavy weight of laws and regulations is transformed into an intensely attractive force that raises the individual from the mire of impenetrable reality to an existence full of purpose and yearning.

Such an individual does not need the threat of punishment or the promise of reward bound up in the imposition of transcendent authority. "He occupies himself with the study of the Law and the fulfillment of the commandments… impelled by no external motive whatsoever, moved neither by fear of calamity nor by the desire to obtain material benefit – such a man does what is truly right because it is truly right, and ultimately happiness comes to him as a result of his conduct" (Maimonides, Laws of Repentance 10:2).

Performing the commandments inspires in him the joy and happiness of creativity. The blurring of the gaps that separate the free personal moral law from the compulsory revelational command causes an experience of total freedom – as if the divine commandment were identical with the demands of the creative rational consciousness. The commandment creates an uninterrupted passageway into secret spiritual foundations, and there man discovers that the revelational commandment actually expresses the longing and heart-stirrings of his hidden existence, which he had not been aware of until now. Man finds the revelational command within himself. Supra-rational necessity joins with the normative consciousness, and together they are absorbed into one ontological/supra-ontological consciousness. It is for this reason that the great Jewish sages were not tormented by the war against their instinctual drives, a war so common in the lives of the gentile sages. Devotion to religious life, even if it begins through compulsion, is maintained out of freedom, joy, and longing. "I will take pleasure in Your commandments, which I have loved; …this is my comfort in my needy state, as your words have given me life" (Ps. 119:47, 50). The revelational statutes are the individual's pleasures and sole comfort. He worships God out of love. [The act of] cleaving to God has absorbed into itself the absolute, supra-rational, supra-natural command.

Is man not exalted by putting on *tefillin*? Does he not feel this exaltation and take pleasure in it? Does man not joyfully experience his *neshamah yeterah* (additional soul) on the Sabbath? Does he not take pleasure in the Sabbath peace and the holiday joy? Does not the fulfillment of the commandments constitute an experience that sweetens the bitterness in man's life, purifies the individual, and redeems him from his distress, loneliness, and grief? Indeed, the more salient the "pointlessness" of the laws, the more heartening the experience.

Chapter Eighteen

A

This outlook has powerful consequences. The creation of the world was a moral act that attained its perfection in the revelation on Mount Sinai. The realization of the moral-revelational imperative constitutes an act of creation; repairing the world constitutes a moral act. In creating the world, the Creator fulfilled the supreme moral purpose. The source of morality is God, and its revelation is creation. The fact of existence is the embodiment of the moral will. A moral act is a creative, innovative act. The supreme human purpose is to live a complete, perfected experience, as well as to take part in elevating the existence of the other. The highest moral good is the totality of what exists: "And God saw all that He had made, and found it very good" (Gen. 1:31). The most terrible evil is privation.

Resembling God, which is the foundation of Jewish morality, is accomplished by imitating His creative acts. Sublime moral life is blended with a creative, active life. One who contributes to perfecting the creation out of longing for the Source of Existence – the living God – raises himself to the supreme moral level. The entire cosmic process is the revelation of the divine morality from out of the faraway realms of enclosure and separation. And whoever intertwines his life and existence with the threads of this cosmic formation through mighty actions, including a renewal of the act of creation in miniature form, and out of a powerful, stormy, seething faith, imitates God and cleaves to Him.

Halakhic Judaism is therefore permeated with total optimism, intoxicated with the fullness and breadth of the world, and devoted to it with all the ardor of its soul. It delights in the bosom of the world and clings to it. Halakhic Judaism is hungry and thirsty for concrete life and its glorious beauty. It hates death and seeks recompense for lives that have become shriveled or dried up before their time and were not properly exploited by man. This is why the Halakhah enjoins that dead bodies be separated from the sacral and the Temple, and why it stresses the importance of the commandment to save human life. Drunk with earthly splendor and swept away by the storm of living, halakhic Judaism protects a reality that is sensible, fresh and variegated. Its motto is "He [God] did not create it [the world] to be chaos; He formed it to be lived in" (Isa. 45:18).

Halakhic Judaism does not separate the eternal from the temporal, or the contingent from the absolute. It does not ignore this world, as other religions do. Every experience is a moral outbreak of infinitude, and the moral purpose of man is to exist in the uniqueness with which God has endowed him. Through this individual existence, in accordance with the requirements of the Halakhah, he will earn eternal life. All the realms of human experience – the qualitative, the quantitative and symbolic (as described by mathematics and physics), the psychobiological, and the normative – relate the glory of the God of morality and give expression to the eternal imperative. The halakhic view does not distinguish between the Kingdom of Heaven and the Kingdom of Earth, but states, "The Kingdom of Heaven is like the Kingdom of Earth" (*Berakhot* 58a) – a kingdom of heaven and earth. "Thus says the Lord: Heaven is My throne, and earth is My footstool" (Isa. 66:1). The existential experience of Judaism does not separate the realms of evil and good, devil and angel, purity and impurity. One realm, which emanates from the radiance of the *Shekhinah*, fills the entire universe. Halakhic Judaism sanctifies the profane, purifies it of the pollution it has absorbed, and refines being of the dross and baseness that human calculations have introduced into it. The entire world is elevated and crowned with a renewed soul, acquires eternal holiness, and unites with its Creator. The boundaries are blurred and disappear; before our eyes is spread out one great creation in which the divine morality is revealed. This creation sings praises to the Creator, the songs of a creature driven by moral longing for its Creator.

B

Judaism does not pursue miracles that occur outside the realm of nature, which have such an important place in the thought of the universal *homo religiosus*. The Jewish sages were uncomfortable about altering the natural way of things. In the Jewish view, miracles and wonders occur only when absolutely necessary, when all other means have been exhausted and man is attacked by his enemies in a place from which he cannot escape. Using a shortcut in the natural realm [even in this case] does not add any glory to the splendor that shines forth from ordered, law-governed reality. On the contrary, it mars the honor of the Creator. The leap from lawful to miraculous revelation is described by the Midrash as a descent, as a degradation of the *Shekhinah* (see *Exodus Rabbah* 15:5). Only because of His great goodness and lovingkindness does God "defile" Himself in order to save His chosen people or punish the wicked. The orderly creation, characterized by monochromatic lawfulness, tells the greatness of God. "The heavens declare the glory of God, the sky proclaims His handiwork" (Ps. 19:2). God's natural Providence is the crowning jewel of His management of the world. Consciousness of Him does not require interruptions of the causal regime.

Philosophical ethics, from its earliest days until Kant and from the time of Kant until the present, has wondered about the connection between moral command and natural law. In other words, it has sought a path from the realm of nature to the moral realm of the spirit. Many pens have been blunted and much ink has been spilled in the attempt to solve the problem of the unity of moral command and natural law. Two philosophical approaches diverged. Some thinkers used the tactic of humanizing ethics, connecting it with anthropological and sociological development, which bounds the moral law within the positivist, utilitarian realm. Others went further afield, to a system of laws and values permeated with baseless absolutism. The transition from ethics to physics and metaphysics remains obscure.

[But] Judaism declares that the only difference between the revelational system of laws and the ontological law is one of perception. The ontological law, which is manifested by the created reality, is revealed to man in the form of the revelational moral command.

The supreme morality is suprahuman. Anthropomorphizing the moral law and connecting it with a sociological process, as many thinkers have done, restricts it to the secular utilitarian realm, thereby destroying the moral world. [For] the moral law is, in essence, the law of existence, and moral action is action interwoven with the drama of the great creation.

C

Not only do the prophets themselves achieve the fulfillment of their longing to cleave to the Divinity, but all Jews can fulfill their aspiration toward God by joining the prophetic tradition. What is this tradition? Prophecy is not only a phenomenon of our past history. The historical revelation that occurred at a particular time remains a living and continuous awareness of the divine revelation, which has been absorbed into the being and singularity of man in all his individuality. The confrontation between God and man, between the Creator and the creature, never ends; the discourse with God is constantly being renewed – in prayer, in transcendent thoughts, and in man's longing emotions. God's revelation is an eternal vision that sails in the stream of time and the flow of the generations.

From the day that God revealed Himself to man, the prophetic vision has not ceased, and God has not departed from man. The God who walked about in the Garden of Eden and called to the first man, "Where are you?" (Gen. 3:9), is still marching in the garden of history and calling to us at times of rage and crisis. The God who said to Abraham, "Go forth from your native land and from your father's house to the land that I will show you" (Gen. 12:1), commands us to leave our comfortable parental homes and the company of our beloved companions and devote ourselves to a sublime aspiration. The God who revealed Himself to Moses from within the burning bush and told him the secret of "I am that I am" (Ex. 3:14) has not disappeared; the bush is still burning, and God's voice from within it resounds in space, relaying the divine mission to all who fight to sanctify God's name. The echo of God's voice is still declaring from Mount Horeb to a world cloaked by desolate, insensitive nature: Who is the second-person "You" who is present and in opposition to whom the "I" of man is individuated? Who is the absent, third-person "He" toward whom both the first-person and the second-person aspire? Who is the "I" [of the revelation] which penetrates natural man and raises the personality within him to the heights of its individuality? Lo, it is the God who both faces and hides from man at the time when He reveals Himself to him. One who does not encounter God cannot be liberated from the gloomy, mute world that has not been illuminated with the light of spiritual uniqueness. Personal reality is the reality of revelation. R. Judah Halevi, the poet-philosopher, discovered this fundamental principle (see *Kuzari*, esp. pt. IV).

God's connection with man has two aspects. On the one hand, God's relationship with the world as a whole includes His relationship with man, for human beings are an inseparable part of the world. On the other hand, He relates to man in and of himself, beyond the rest of the universe, with a relationship of both uniqueness and revelation. At this stage, man becomes one with his Creator and also one with himself as a human "subject." God's revelation to man and man's revelation to himself as a human entity are simultaneous. As R. Judah Halevi expressed it, the Creator reveals Himself with the name Elokim as the possessor of powers relating to the natural world (*Kuzari* IV:1), a world which is nothing but [an impersonal] system of mechanical forces, and to closed-off natural man, who constitutes an infinitesimal fraction of this world. The Creator reveals Himself to spiritual man with His special name, the Tetragrammaton, as the "I" at Mount Sinai. When the infinite "I" connects with man, man is redeemed from a closed-off natural existence and is raised to a unique personal level of existence.

Before man was created, the world was separated from the mystery of God as "Elokim"; once man was created, the secret of God's complete name was revealed, and the Torah began using the [compound] name "Hashem Elokim." Afterwards the Kabbalists said that living souls have their basis and their secret in this complete name of God (as per the expression of our Sages, "A full name over a full universe" [*Gen. Rabbah* 13:3]). This is God's singular name, which symbolizes the mystical stature of the mysterious divine emanation from the sphere of Wisdom (*Hokhmah*) to the sphere of Kingship (*Malkhut*). The hidden Infinite clothes itself in this name when it reveals itself in its uniqueness of personality and selfhood. When the Creator thus reveals Himself in this unique personal revelation, man is granted personal uniqueness and the opportunity to stand before God. This establishes two sorts of relations between the individual and God: a second-person "I-Thou" relation and a third-person "I-He" relation. The divine revelation lifts the individual up from the level of a living creature to the level of an intellectual, speaking being, from object to person, from a closed-off creature to an open one. This revelation never comes to an end, since if it were to cease, the unique personal consciousness of the individual would come to an end. "The Lord spoke those words to your whole congregation at the mountain, out of the fire and the dense clouds, in a mighty voice that did not cease" (Deut. 5:19). "I make this covenant… not with you alone, but both with those who are standing here with us this day… and with those who are not here with us this day" (Deut. 29:13–14). The Midrash says that every last soul of the Jewish people, to the end of all the generations, stood at the foot of Mount Sinai at the time when the *Shekhinah* revealed itself (*Pirkei de-Rabbi Eliezer* 41), and the Kabbalists ascribed a special significance to this tradition. The revelation of the *Shekhinah* is torn loose like a sandbank, carried upon the waves of the flow of time.

❧ Chapter Nineteen

The Heart That Runs Without Returning

*"Let me be a seal upon your heart, like the
seal upon your arm" (Song 8:6).*

A

The Halakhah adorned this marvelous idea of the perpetuation of the revelation of the *Shekhinah* and of the word of God, calling it the transmission and a reception of the Oral Torah. These terms do not denote merely the technical act of parents telling their children about the laws and the *halakhot*, or teachers relating them to their students – a faithful historical-information service. The transmission and reception of the Oral Torah convey a broader and deeper concept than that. They are embodied in the infusion of the revelational consciousness, in the transmission of the vision of the living God, through an experience that rages from one generation to the next. The generations are united, and eras are joined in one point at the focus of the revelation.

The purpose of reading the Torah aloud in the synagogue is not solely to teach the congregation, but also to arrange an encounter with God, as experienced by our ancestors at Mount Sinai. Every act of reading from the Torah is a new giving of the Torah, a revival of the wondrous stand at the foot of the flaming mountain. The reading of the Torah is a "staging" of the giving of the Torah and a renewal of the awesome, sublime experience. The revelational experience is reenacted whenever the Torah scroll is removed from the ark [for reading in the synagogue]. The person who is called up to the Torah utters a formula of sanctification ("Bless the blessed Lord") before the prescribed benediction. Why does he not simply begin with the benediction itself? The reading of the Torah contains an element of revelation of the *Shekhinah*, and whenever or wherever man feels the presence of the Holy One, Blessed Be He, he is obligated to sanctify God's name and praise Him: "Then shall all the trees of the forest shout for joy at the presence of the Lord, for He is coming, for He is coming to rule the earth" (1 Chron. 16:33).

R. Meir of Rothenburg's stringency of standing during the synagogue reading of the Torah is based on this principle. If the public reading of the Torah were merely an educational activity, there would be no need to stand. Since the time of Rabban Gamliel the Elder, we sit while studying the Torah (*Megillah* 21a). Standing is an outcome of the revelational experience. Another corollary of this principle is the custom that the synagogue reading of the Ten Commandments uses the "higher" cantillation (*ta'am elyon*), which combines all the verses of each commandment into one verse, in contrast to the "lower" cantillation, which organizes them by individual verses. Through this practice we are "imitating" the way God Himself uttered the commandments. When He made the commandment heard, the only sentential unit was the whole commandment. The unit of the individual verse had no place. When we are studying the commandments, in contrast, we read each verse as a separate unit. When the Written Torah is studied, it is divided only into units of individual verses.

Moreover, even when the Torah is studied by individuals, there is an element of the revelation of the *Shekhinah*. The Talmud puts it this way:

It is taught: [The verse (Deut. 4:9) states,] "Make them known to your children and to your children's children," and afterwards [in the next verse] it is written, "The day you stood before the Lord your God at Horeb." Just as at that time [you were] in terror and awe and trembling and quaking, so too in this case [you should be] in terror and awe and trembling and quaking (*Berakhot* 22a).[22]

A master who has heard the Torah is filled with living, revelational content. He impresses his disciples not only by narrating and understanding the vision as an intellectual act, but also by uniting spiritually with them and by bestowing of his personal glory upon them. Prophecies were absorbed into the being of the prophet, and when he transmitted the prophecies to his disciples, he granted them some of his essence. Thus, the transmission of prophecies is also a transmission of the soul and the spirit, one soul linking with the other, and one spirit cleaving to the other. [In the Sinai desert, when God suggested that Moses share the burdens of leadership with seventy elders, He said to him,] "I will come down and speak with you there, and I will draw upon the spirit that is on you and put it upon them" (Num. 11:17). [Later on, when Moses was about to die and sought a successor, God told him,] "Single out Joshua son of Nun, an inspired man, and lay your hand upon him. Have him stand before Eleazar the priest and before the whole community, and commission him in their sight. Invest him with some of your glory" (Num. 27:18–20). The Holy One, Blessed Be He, bestowed upon the seventy elders some of the Holy Spirit that had dwelt upon the master prophet. Moses granted some of his original personal splendor and glory to Joshua. In this bestowal of spirit and granting of glory, some of Moses's personal uniqueness was also transmitted to his disciples.

When the world emanates from the Infinite, it draws the divine *Shekhinah* along with it, because it is impossible for an existent thing to emanate from God's bosom without the divine *Shekhinah* clinging to it (this is the exile of the *Shekhinah*). So too is it impossible for a prophet to relate his prophecies to others, or for a Torah scholar to teach Torah to others, without the giver's personality touching that of the receivers. The act of a master teaching Torah to his students is a wondrous metaphysical act of the revelation of the influencing personality to the one influenced by it. This revelation is also the cleaving of teacher and student to each other. The student who understands a concept cleaves to the intellect that transmits the concept. If he grasps the teacher's logic, then he becomes joined to the teacher in the unity of the conceiving intellect (*maskil*) and the conceived ideas (*muskal*).

Within this fundamental principle is hidden the secret of the Oral Torah, a Torah which by its nature and application can never be objectified, even after it has been written down. "Oral Torah" means a Torah that blends with the individual's personal uniqueness and becomes an inseparable part of man. When the person then transmits it to someone else, his personal essence is transmitted along with it. Even the Written Torah, although given to Moses in a specific, fixed format, and even though there is a commandment to write it in black ink on parchment, adheres to those who study it and becomes one with them. When someone teaches Torah to another, the giver emits something of his essence to the receiver. One's Torah disciples are called one's children (*Sifrei* 34 [to Deut. 6:7]) because the essence of their spiritual personality emanates, and is born, from the bosom of the teacher. The Torah therefore established stricter rules for honoring one's Torah teachers than for honoring one's parents, because whereas one's parents bring one into the life of the mundane world in that they cause one's bodily and mental existence, one's Torah teachers bring one to the heights of a spiritual world that is much more sublime (*Bava Metzi'a* 33a).

The Torah teacher is always revealed from within the depths of his faithful disciple's soul. The prophets and sages of the Jewish people burst forth from the depths of the nation's historical consciousness. The souls of the first generations following the revelation have been transmitted in the course of the centuries until they are absorbed in the recesses of the historical reality of the Jewish community that yearns for redemption. The *Shekhinah* speaks out of the throat of the destitute, reviled, and abandoned "last generation" (Deut. 29:21). If this generation so wills it, the revelation is not a vague, ancient vision, but a fresh, living one, effervescent in its being and expressed in the consciousness of eternal awe and yearning. When the Halakhah discusses the transmission of the Torah, the receiving of the tradition (*masorah*), it is not dealing with an abstract idea, but with something real that urges, yearns, and impels the individual to activity.

I would like to relate a personal experience to illustrate the idea of the *masorah* that we are discussing.

I remember myself as a child, a lonely, forlorn boy. I was afraid of the world. It seemed cold and alien. I felt as if everyone were mocking me. But I had one friend, and he was – please don't laugh at me – Maimonides, the Rambam. How did we become friends? We simply met!

The Rambam was a regular guest in our house. Those were the days when my father, my mentor, was still living in the home of my grandfather, the great and pious Rabbi Elijah Feinstein of Pruzhna. Father sat and studied Torah day and night. A rather small group of outstanding young Torah scholars gathered around him and imbibed his words thirstily.

Father's lectures were given in my grandfather's living room, where my bed was placed. I used to sit up in bed and listen to my father talk. My father always spoke about the Rambam. This is how he would proceed: He would open a volume of the Talmud and read a passage. Then he would say, "This is the interpretation of Rabbi Isaac and the [other] Tosafists; now let us see how the Rambam interpreted the passage." Father would always find that the Rambam had offered a different interpretation and had deviated from the simple way. My father would say, almost as a complaint against the Rambam, "We don't understand our Master's reasoning or the way he explains the passage." It was as if he were complaining to the Rambam directly, "Rabbenu Mosheh, why did you do this?"

My father would then say that, *prima facie*, the criticisms and objections of the Rabad are actually correct. The members of the group would jump up and each of them would suggest an idea. Father would listen and rebut their ideas, and then repeat, "Our Master's words are as hard to crack as iron." But he would not despair; he would rest his head on his fist and sink into deep thought. The group was quiet and did not disturb his reflections. After a long while he would lift his head very slowly and begin, "*Rabbotai*, let's see…" and then he would start to talk. Sometimes he would say a great deal, other times only a little. I would strain my ears and listen to what he was saying.

I did not understand anything at all about the issue under discussion, but two impressions were formed in my young, innocent mind: (1) the Rambam was surrounded by opponents and "enemies" who want to harm him; and (2) his only defender was my father. If not for my father, who knew what would happen to the Rambam? I felt that the Rambam himself was present in the living room, listening to what my father was saying. The Rambam was sitting with me on my bed. What did he look like? I didn't know exactly, but his countenance resembled my father's good and beautiful face. He had the same name as my father – Moses. Father would speak; the students, their eyes fixed on him, would listen intently to what he was saying. Slowly, slowly, the tension ebbed; Father strode boldly and bravely. New arguments emerged; halakhic rules were formulated and defined with wondrous precision. A new light shone. The difficulties were resolved, the passage was explained. The Rambam emerged the winner. Father's face shone with joy. He had defended his "friend," Rabbenu Mosheh the son of Maimon. A smile of satisfaction appeared on the Rambam's lips. I too participated in this joy. I was happy and excited. I would jump out of bed and run to my mother's room to tell her the joyful news, "Mother, Mother, the Rambam is right, he defeated the Rabad. Father came to his aid. How wonderful Father is!"

But occasionally the Rambam's luck did not hold – his "enemies" attacked him on all sides; the difficulties were as hard as iron. Father was unable to follow the logic of his position. He tried with all his might to defend him, but he was unsuccessful. Father would sink into musings with his head leaning on his fist. The students and I, and even the Rambam himself, would tensely wait for Father's answer. But Father would pick up his head and say sadly, "The answer will have to wait for the prophet Elijah; what the Rambam says is extremely difficult. There is no expert who can explain it. The issue remains in need of clarification." The whole group, my father included, were sad to the point of tears. A silent agony expressed itself on each face. Tears came from my eyes, too. I would even see bright teardrops in the Rambam's eyes.

Slowly I would go to Mother and tell her with a broken heart, "Mother, Father can't resolve the Rambam – what should we do?"

"Don't be sad," Mother would answer, "Father will find a solution for the Rambam. And if he doesn't find one, then maybe when you grow up you'll resolve his words. The main thing is to learn Torah with joy and excitement."

This experience belongs to my childhood. Still, it is not the golden fantasy of a little boy; the feeling in it is not mystical. It is a completely historical, psychological reality that is alive even now in the depths of my soul. When I sit down to learn Torah, I find myself immediately in the company of the sages of the *masorah*. The relations between us are personal. The Rambam is at my right, Rabbenu Tam at my left, Rashi sits up front and interprets, Rabbenu Tam disputes him; the Rambam issues a ruling, and the Rabad objects. They are all in my little room, sitting around my table. They look at me affectionately, enjoy arguing and studying the Talmud with me, encourage and support me the way a father does. Torah study is not solely an educational activity. It is not a merely formal, technical matter embodied in the discovery and exchange of facts. It is a powerful experience of becoming friends with many generations of Torah scholars, the joining of one spirit with another, the union of souls. Those who transmitted the Torah and those who received it come together in one historical way-station.

Thus, the Rambam remained my friend even after my childhood, and we are friends to this very day. Indeed, there is only one difference between my childhood experience and my present one. In my childhood, only the Rambam was my friend, while at present my study group has grown and includes many Torah scholars. All the sages of the tradition, from the days of Moses to the present, have become my friends! When I solve a problem in the Rambam's or Rabbenu Tam's writings, I see their glowing faces expressing their satisfaction. I always feel as if the Rambam and Rabbenu Tam are kissing me on the forehead and shaking my hand. This is not a fantasy. It is a very deep experience. It is the experience of the transmission of the Oral Torah.

The teaching and transmitting of Torah and transmitting the Torah glow with the attribute of *hesed*, lovingkindness, with which God created the world. Just as God acts with lovingkindness toward the world, so must the prophet act toward his fellow humans. If the prophet's mind has been "intertwined" with the Infinite and "connected" with the mind of the Creator, he must realize that he is the main conduit through which plenitude from the Eternal flows toward human beings. A man of God who has attained the level of a mental connection just below the divine throne and of cleaving to the living God, cannot remain alone with himself and live separately from society. This would be as if a rich miser, to whom God granted great wealth in order that he become a benefactor to the downtrodden and miserable members of his faith, had betrayed this trust and kept all the wealth for himself.

Neither prophecy nor wisdom is the property of the individual; they belong to everyone. Prophets and wise men are appointed as guardians for the distribution of spiritual wealth. Prophets who keep their prophecy to themselves are deserving of death meted out by Heaven, since they are considered to have betrayed their mission. Just as God revealed Himself through His actions from the hidden, separated Infinite, clothing Himself in the benevolent act of expansion and thus creating the world, so must the prophet reveal himself to others from within the closed-off isolation of the self. He must open all the treasures of his soul to them, until the wisdom of the prophet's vision adheres to his listeners and the prophecy is transmitted in its original form to the others who participate in the divine vision through this act of transmission.

Prophecy is transmitted through the benevolent whisper of the prophet's existential coupling with the other, the individual's merging with the community. The prophet's consciousness expands and absorbs everything into itself. It shares the revelational vision with society. The truth of the prophecy fills the prophet's entire being, bubbling up and overflowing its banks and bursting out of the recesses of the mind like a mighty waterfall that sweeps everything away in its flood. Here there is no demarcation of existences into the "I" and the "thou"; the domains are interwoven, and the existences blend into one another. There emerges a community-self that sees the divine visions. The current of mercy floods not only the prophesying "I" and the "thou" who listens to the prophet directly, but also the "he" of the faraway individual. The prophet pours some of his being into the generations that are to come, the minds that have not yet emerged from the dark of nothingness, the last generation hidden in the fog of the unknown future. The "community of Israel" means the coupling of the first and the last generations of prophet and listener, Torah teacher and disciple, the revelation of the *Shekhinah* in the dim light of the dawn and the vision of the end of days at the appointed time. The community of Israel, which is also the congregation of Israel, includes within itself the faithful ancient evidence (the word for congregation [*edah*] being related to the word for testimony [*edut*]) of the visions that have not sunk into the abyss of the past, of the continuity of history and the transmission of the revelation from one generation to the next.

The individual and the community must come together through an act of historical identification with the past and future, the fate and destiny, of the Jewish people. The vision of the beginning and the end is constantly being renewed and joins the individual and community from past generations of *Keneset Yisrael* with those to come. Thus can the individual cleave completely and absolutely to God in an attachment that no longer involves either flight or retreat.

ぶ Chapter Twenty
Summary

*A*ctive participation in the work of reconstructing the content of revelation is the goal of Judaism as it wends its way through the three layers of transcendent consciousness. From a state of trust alternating with fear, it evolves into a state of love combined with awe, and from there it climbs up to a state of love characterized by desire and cleaving.

At first, human questioning brings man to the revelational encounter. Through his striving for the absolute, for the noncontingent and the eternal, he encounters the divine command and the supranatural authority that demand of him to follow a particular way of life. The revelational experience on this level denies and contradicts man's intellectual values and aspires to replace the free activity of man's spirit with the passivity of compulsion and anxiety.

In the second stage, man begins to befriend the revelational experience and to feel trust in it; he tries to link it to his experience of God within the system of lawful and orderly nature; he identifies with the consciousness of the God of the world, which expresses the wonder of lovingkindness, compassion, and blessings, as well as with the consciousness of a God above and beyond the world, which demands absolute subjugation and commitment from the individual. This stage includes aspects of imperative subjugation and revelation, with all the weight of the supra-rational authority that oppresses man's consciousness; but it also includes the serenity of complete trust and the expectation of absolute reward. Man performs God's commandments against his will; but as a side effect of the compulsion, he feels the complete tranquility of the slave who does his master's bidding, and the revelation thereby provides support for the wanderer in the paths of the creation. The goal is to imitate God. It includes aspects of necessity as well as aspects of joy and security.

The imperative nature of man's behavior gradually palls at the dawn of the third stage, the stage combining love with awe, when the soul longs for its Creator out of the aspiration for total attachment and strives to achieve this in a running movement without any retreat. While the goal in the second stage is to imitate God, the end of the third stage is to cleave to Him. What is the difference between the two aims? Imitating God includes aspects of total freedom and total subjugation. Cleaving is entirely free activity. Man lives according to the Torah and the commandments in great joy. He desires to do the will of God as if the will of the Infinite were also the will of the finite individual. In the third stage we see the wonder of the identification of wills.

ঌ Notes

1. The allegorical character of the Song of Songs is a firm principle of the Halakhah, upon which are founded both the physical sanctity of the scroll of the Song of Songs as not to be touched (it "defiles the hands" [*Yadayim* 3:5]), and the sanctity of the name Shelomoh [Solomon], occurrences of which in the Song of Songs are interpreted allegorically as appellations for God [*Shelomoh* = *Melekh she-ha-shalom shelo*, "the King to whom peace belongs"]. The aggadic tradition interprets the Song of Songs symbolically.

However, there is a dual allegorical interpretation, one metaphysical-historical and the other metaphysical-universal. The first interprets the book as a duet sung by the Holy One, Blessed Be He, and the community of Israel that bursts forth from the history of this nation; the second tends to expound it as material for the duet sung by God and humankind in general, expressing the mutual longings of Creator and created.

The Midrash and the Targum [the Aramaic translation of the Bible] affirm the historical view. This is the interpretation offered by Rashi, R. Judah Halevi, Ibn Ezra, and others. Maimonides, on the other hand, following Rabbenu Bahya, took the universalist position:

> What is the love of God that is befitting? It is to love the Eternal with a great and exceeding love...like a love-sick man whose mind is at no time free from his passion for a certain woman.... The entire Song of Songs is indeed an allegory descriptive of this love (*Mishneh Torah*, Laws of Repentance 10:3).

Maimonides offered a similar explanation in *Guide of the Perplexed* III:51. The Kabbalists followed him in this interpretation.

In truth, both interpretations refer to the same basic idea: the relationship between God and the world. This connection, however, is expressed in two ways: between God and the individual, and between God and the collective. Just as God longs to cleave to the individual, He also desires to perpetuate His dwelling within a singular collective, a chosen community and a unique nation. The tension is two-sided, being at once universalist and suprahistorical, but also national and historical. In his *Epistle to Yemen*, Maimonides used a quotation from the Song of Songs to describe the Jewish people's historical fate. The Kabbalists joined the two motifs – the world and the Jewish people – in their exposition of the book; in their view, it hints at the mutual longings of the *Malka Kadisha* [Holy King] and the *Shekhinah* [divine presence]. On the one hand, the *Shekhinah* symbolizes God's presence within the world; on the other, it symbolizes the community of Israel, in which the majesty of the Holy One, Blessed Be He, is revealed. The Song of Songs is both a book belonging to the whole world and the singular book of the community of Israel.

The Mishnah (*Yadayim* 3:5) calls the Song of Songs the holy of holies:

> Rabbi Akiva said, "No Jew has ever denied, God forbid, that the scroll of the Song of Songs makes one's hands impure [a distinguishing characteristic of all the canonical books of the Bible], for the whole world has never been as worthy as on the day that the Song of Songs was given to the community of Israel, for all the books of the Bible are holy, but the Song of Songs is the holy of holies."

The description of the Song of Songs as the holy of holies refers to the divine symbolism in it. However, it also expresses a halakhic principle: The book cannot be interpreted according to its plain sense (*peshat*). In all the rest of the Torah, we are permitted to interpret the verses according to either the midrashic reading or the plain reading. The plain meaning constitutes an entity of Torah. In the Song of Songs, however, the literal reading is excluded from [being invested with] the status of Torah. Its place has been taken by the midrashic reading. In this case, the symbolic method is the only one we can use. Anyone who explains this book, in accordance with the literal meaning of the words, as referring to sensual love, defiles its sanctity and denies the Oral Torah.

We find this principle in Maimonides' introduction to his *Commentary on the Mishnah* with reference to other interpretations. There is a singular type of interpretation, received from Moses at Sinai, that no one is permitted to dispute. In these cases, only the rabbinic explicatory interpretation (*derashah*) exists; the plain meaning has been completely abolished. To interpret literally such verses as "and you must cut off her hand" (Deut. 25:12), "an eye for an eye" (Ex. 21:24), and "the fruit of a goodly tree" (Lev. 23:40) constitutes denial of our tradition. (See *Bava Kamma* 84a: "R. Eliezer says: 'An eye for an eye' literally. Do you really think so? Does R. Eliezer dispute all the other Tannaim?")

None of the sages involved in transmitting the Oral Torah may deviate from the received interpretation. Maimonides puts it this way in his introduction to the Mishnah:

> This is the basic principle: You must understand the secret, that the interpretations received by Moses cannot be subject to controversy. From that time until now, we have not found any controversy among the sages at any time, from the days of Moses until the days of R. Ashi, such that one sage would say, "If someone puts out another person's eye, his eye must be put out, because the verse says 'An eye for an eye,' while another sage would say, "He need give only an indemnity." Nor have we found a controversy about the Torah verse "The fruit of a goodly tree," which is [interpreted as being] a citron, where someone would say that it is a quince or a pomegranate or something else.

See also Maimonides' *Mishneh Torah*, Laws of Damages and Injuries 1:1–3; *Sanhedrin* 101a: "Anyone who reads a verse of the Song of Songs and turns it into a lyric brings evil into the world...for the Torah dons sackcloth and complains to the Holy One, Blessed Be He" (*Avot de-Rabbi Natan* 36; *Zohar*, II, 144a; *Shevu'ot* 35b; *Megillah* 7a).

2. I would like to call the reader's attention to one thing in order to prevent misunderstanding on the part of those who study our master's [Maimonides'] teachings in depth. Love in Aristotelian philosophy is one-way: the world yearns for the Prime Mover, without experiencing reciprocal love. The Prime Mover is aloof from the world and does not long for it. His relationship to the world is that of a teleological

and necessary cause, without desire or intention. Since there is no directed providence in Aristotle's view, the love of the Prime Mover for the world is abolished. Moreover, the world's love for the pure form is not an intentional act but an immanent function that sets the cosmic process into motion.

The Torah, which bases all of Judaism on the principle of creation and providence, but also on the principle of the chosenness of the Jewish people, introduced into the center of our world the concept of loving-kindness and of love as a reciprocal process. The creation of the world is the embodiment of God's grace. God's providence over His creatures in general, and His choice of the congregation of Israel in particular, is a manifestation of infinite love. Anyone who says that Judaism commands the individual to love God but does not promise him reciprocal love is a heretic. How unfortunate it is that many scholars pursued folly and suspected that Maimonides, Heaven forbid, agreed with the teaching of Aristotelian philosophy that the yearnings of the world for God are one-way, without any reciprocal yearnings.

Maimonides does indeed say the following in *Guide of the Perplexed*:

> We have already made it clear to you that that intellect which over-flowed from Him, may He be exalted, toward us is the bond between us and Him. You have the choice: if you wish to strengthen and fortify this bond, you can do so; if, however, you wish gradually to make it weaker and feebler until you cut it, you can also do that (III:51).

As a result, many scholars claimed that God does not care about maintaining a love relationship between Himself and His creatures. But such an interpretation is wrong, and locating the error does not require deep investigation. The principle of free will makes it necessary for man to have the ability to loosen his ontic link with God. If people can sin, why can't they abolish God's love for them? But there is not even the slightest hint here of a lack of divine love.

The books of the Torah and the Prophets are replete with descriptions of God's love for Israel: "God willed not to listen to Balaam...because God loves you" (Deut. 23:6); "But God desired your ancestors for love of them, and chose their descendants" (Deut. 10:15); "He judges the orphan and the widow, and loves the alien, giving him food and clothing" (Deut. 10:18); "He is distressed in all of their distress, and the angel who goes before Him redeems them in His love and compassion" (Isa. 63:9); "I have loved you, says God…and I love Jacob" (Mal. 1:2). A special blessing was established to be uttered before reading the *Shema*, beginning with "Eternal love" or "Great love," and ending with "He who loves His nation Israel." The special blessing for the holiness of the day, which contains the idea of Israel's chosenness, is coined in terms of love: "You have chosen us from all the nations, you have loved us and wanted us." If this love ceases, then Providence ceases as well, and so, too, does Israel's chosenness.

In truth, the attribute of mercy is the attribute of love: "I will love You, O Lord, my strength" (Ps. 18:2) [the verb *rahem* is here understood as "love," because of the unsuitability of its usual meaning, "to have mercy"]. Moreover, the standard Aramaic translation of Onkelos renders "You shall love your God" with the Aramaic form of *rahem*. Maimonides himself mentions the attribute of love in many places in his code of Jewish law: "…because God loves us and is keeping his vow to our Father Abraham" (Laws of Idolatry 1:3); "God Himself loves *gerim* [converts to Judaism], as it is written, 'And He loves the *ger*'" (Laws of Character Traits 6:4); "Great is repentance, for it brings one near to the *Shekhinah*…. Yesterday he was hated by the Deity, abhorred and distanced from Him, and today he is beloved, desirable, and a close friend…. Moreover, they [penitents] are eagerly desired" (Laws of Repentance 7:6–7). Maimonides calls the second book of his code "The Book of Love." It is unimaginable that Maimonides, the pillar of the Halakhah, was influenced in a fundamental issue like this by Arabic philosophical inquiry, which was somewhat affected by Aristotle's view.

In truth, it is necessary to study Maimonides' theory of attributes (especially the affective attributes [Ex. 34:6–7]) in order to understand God's love for His creatures. However, halakhic thought does not demand that love be an attribute unto itself; nor does it need it. It can make do with the little that means a lot: the attributes of action on which is based Jewish morality, which considers God the source of moral existence. Were this love to have the status of one of the attributes of the Almighty that were revealed to Moses at the time of mercy and divine favor, and which teach us the principles of human morality – this would be enough for us! If the Creator's behavior toward His world reflects the pure lights of infinite love, then from our point of view we have attained our ultimate purpose.

On the other hand, the ancient moral principle of subjugating the psyche to the intellect took on a completely different form in Maimonides' system. It does aspire to deny affective life in its many and variegated colors, as the Stoics aspired to do in their day when they delineated the supreme theoretical man [the *sophos*, sage], or even to impose upon it a one-way formal regime, as was Aristotle's dream. What Maimonides wanted to do was to establish an enduring conjunction of the psyche with the intellect. Reason conjoins with emotion and is enriched by it. Reason supports emotion but is also nourished by it; there is reciprocity here. On the one hand, when the affects blend with the intellect, their nature changes, and they become less passive. In place of involuntary impressions, free activity blossoms. When cognition absorbs emotion, it converts it and subsumes it under free action and creation. Cognition bestows some of its glory onto emotion – the glory of free action and the desire for accomplishment. On the other hand, cognition too is elevated through its melding with emotionality. The unity of the knower and the known, which is one of the main principles of Maimonides' theory (*Guide* 1:68), occurs only in a cognition imbued with love and desire. Even though Maimonides wrote a great deal about the worthlessness of a primitive, unrestrained emotional life and recommended the rule of the intellect, he nevertheless, following Bahya, set forth love as the goal of divine worship. There is an identity of love and cognition: "One only loves God with the knowledge with which one knows Him. According to the knowledge will be the love. If the former be little or much, so will the latter be little or much" (Laws of Repentance 10:6).

Many aspects of this view influenced the modern theory of affects that is now so prevalent in phenomenological epistemology, and which draws upon the idea of "the logic of the heart" (*logique du coeur*).

Instead of discussing the logic of the heart, however, Maimonides focuses on the emotional heart of logic. Intellectual cognition throws off sparks of active, effervescent emotion. There is no need to go into the details of this epistemological innovation, which is so important for understanding the human essence and for grounding the unity of the individual. We have discussed this innovation a bit, as it greatly elucidates the problem of divine love. When Maimonides transformed the concept of understanding from a passive compulsion to a free activity, he also removed emotionality from the situation of an affect – an unavoidable impression and involuntary instinctive reaction imbued in Man-as-Nature – to the wide-open expanses of free activity born of reason and form nourished by Man-as-Spirit. He thus discovered something about the knowledge of the Eternal. Within His infinite knowledge, identical with the Supreme Will, is ensconced as well His free, creative love – there is no knowledge without active will and active love. The unity of the knower and the known champions love.

The mutual love between God and the community of Israel served as the main motif for the composition of *piyyutim* [special poetic prayers] for the Sabbaths during the counting of the days of the Omer. Echoes of Song of Songs burst forth from these prayers. Love as a cosmic metaphysical principle was emphasized by all the Jewish sages, especially [Hasdai] Crescas and Judah Abravanel.

3. The proofs so prevalent in both general and Jewish philosophy attest to the human longing for God. These demonstrations can be divided into five categories. As mentioned in the text, we do not need these demonstrations as proofs, because the experience of God is the basis of certainty.

(1) The supreme cosmological proof, from the world to its Creator, completely dominated medieval philosophy. It is based on the concept of the First Cause or the Final End.

(2) The teleological proof, in accordance with the definition of causality offered by Aristotle and his followers, coincided with the cosmological one, since in this view the difference between cause and end is purely nominal. Once the classical physics of Newton and Galileo, with its notion of mechanical causality, appeared on the scene, a split occurred and the two demonstrations were divided into two separate conceptions. The teleological demonstration is used by all those who are taken by the biologistic, neovitalistic worldview and influenced by such thinkers as [Henri] Bergson, the brothers [John and Richard] Haldane, and [Hans] Driesch.

(3) The ontological proof infers the existence of an absolutely transcendent reality, not from cosmic events, but from the idea itself. With some changes of both form and content, this demonstration became dominant in the modern rationalistic philosophy of such thinkers as [René] Descartes, [Benedict] Spinoza, [Gottfried] Leibniz, and [Christian] Wolff.

Proofs (1)–(3) all make use of either the external world or the idea itself to reach God.

(4) Another approach has emerged in the field of theological

inquiry. The experience of the self, with all its depths, contradictions, and marvels, reflects the image of the Creator latent within the individual's personality. This view, which draws upon the "image of God" in Genesis (see *Berakhot* 10a), and which was already known to R. Sa'adyah Gaon, is the central pillar of the Pietist movement and religious Romanticism, on the one hand, and the theories of Kant and the neo-Kantians, on the other. The ethical approach of Kant and his followers, the affective approach of [Friedrich] Schleiermacher, and similar views seek traces of God in the depths of the soul in many and varied ways, without needing to make use of the causal cosmic order. It is superfluous to stress that the subjectivist schools in religion ([Søren] Kierkegaard, [Auguste] Sabatier, [Jakob] Hermann) followed this approach.

(5) Contemporary philosophy adopted another view, rooted in the teachings of the mystics, who base their transcendental experience upon a *sui generis* religious factuality. Man feels the presence of God in an unmediated way. The Eternal, just like the sensible, can be directly felt and immediately experienced.

4. Actually, Maimonides' remarks in his *Mishneh Torah*, Laws of the Foundations of the Torah (1:1), are directed at this theory:

> The basic principle of all basic principles and the pillar of all sciences is to realize that there is a First Existent who brought every existing thing into being. All existing things, whether celestial, terrestrial, or belonging to an intermediate class, exist only through His true existence.

This knowledge is not based on logical inference, but is, rather, immediate: the knowledge of reality as divine reality, the awareness of the creation as something separated from the bosom of the Infinite. Even though Maimonides did not desist from presenting indirect demonstrations of the existence of God, and even though he believed that proofs of this sort exhaust our knowledge of the First Existent, the essence of his view is nevertheless that this knowledge is based on the immediate ontological cognition that there is no reality but God. This is the new teaching that was given to Moses with the statement "I am that I am" (Ex. 3:14), as Maimonides interpreted it: I exist necessarily, and any attribution of existence is only a metaphor for My infinite existence, whose necessity is its essence [essence = truth = existence] (*Guide* 1:63). True existence is divine existence, and everything that exists "depends on it" for its existence. This theory is one of the most wonderful and profound thoughts that our great teacher put at the center of his world.

5. Maimonides expresses this as follows:

> But sometimes truth flashes out to us so that we think that it is day, and then matter and habit in their various forms conceal it so that we find ourselves again in an obscure light, almost as we were at first. We are like someone in a very dark night over whom lightning flashes time and time again (*Guide of the Perplexed*, Introduction).

6. But occasionally a mad spirit blows in the world. The contingent and the temporal reject the absolute and eternal and rebel against it. A tidal wave of heresy confronts religion to destroy it. The secular worldview, bereft of God, conquers wide domains, countries and nations. Although even skeptics cannot deny that which is wondrous and hidden from them, they enjoy their mental and spiritual torment. A mania of masochism masters them utterly. They want to remain alone, by themselves, in a mechanical world without meaning or purpose, bereft of joy and hope. Atheists wander along the paths of an absurd existence. They are lost in their absurd, cruel agony and madness.

7. Do not consider this a trivial issue, and do not scorn the transcendent experience based on it. The entire essence of science is the mind's "response" to the question of sensation, the clash between the concept and the mystery of feeling. Every school of epistemology, whether it champions the intellect or sides with the cause of the senses, has been forced to admit, on the one hand, that science is a creation that uses the categories of logic – the free innovations of the mind – but, on the other, that it is the echo of the senses, which "stimulate" cognition. Just as it is impossible to create a scientific world out of *a priori* reason (Hegel failed in his attempt to do this), so is it impossible to devise a scientific theory that is nourished only by the concrete provisions of the sensations. This fundamental rule, which has been discussed endlessly by researchers since the days of Greek philosophy, was given a proper epistemological formulation in Kant's theory. The many attempts that emerged in the field of philosophy, whether of idealist epistemologies that went too far

and tried to enhance the importance of the intellect and lessen that of the senses, or of those which exaggerated the importance of sensation and rebelled against the rule of the mind, did not last very long. The human mind has not yet defined a monistic principle that could ground epistemology. Science is stuck fast in the dualism of sensation and reason, and will never be able to move out of it.

Let us therefore consider the question: On what is the dualism of sensation and conception based? The former is the mystery, the eternal question, while the latter is the answer, the solution! But does reason really solve the problem of the senses? Does it give an account of sensible reality and go deep into the mystery of "pure" qualia (sensory qualities) that leaps upon the individual unawares and willy-nilly? Let us return to our previous discussion to elucidate this important thesis. It is true that the senses ask and the mind answers, but the answer is not relevant to the question. The senses demand a solution to the riddle of real, vital, flowing qualia, while the mind responds with an ideal, quantitative construction that is dumb to reality and closed off to purposefulness. The senses hint at a world full of motion, change, and form, swept along in a mighty, many-colored stream, while pure reason creates abstract, formal objects, bereft of vitality and tumult, whose existence is rooted not in their essence and independence, but in their mutual interrelations. Mathematical physics regards the sensible world as an eternal enigma.

I will now recapitulate my preceding remarks. Instead of explaining the system of qualia from within its own unique self, science creates a new, ideal symbolic system parallel to it. It flees from qualia that flow from one unknown to another, creating a new world fettered in mutual relations and functional dependencies. Even though science then returns to the qualitative and measures its ideal new theories against the standard of sense perception because the free symbols have to conform to the vital qualitative cues, nevertheless there remains the mystery of the variegated sights and sounds that excite everything and smile at everything. The *logos* does not consort with [this mystery]. It does not penetrate the shell of the nonrational senses, and does not form a unity of cognition with it. For example, when I perceive a color, the qualitative riddle, the question, emerges. But what is the answer? The wavelength, a mathematical quantity. The answer does not explain the qualitative content. Science has found a correlative, an exact parallel in the natural order of quantity. There is a parallelism here between the two series, the qualitative and the quantitative. But there is no explanation. We know precisely that the objective, quantitative order matches the subjective, qualitative one. But this match does not answer or solve the question "What is the qualitative nature of the color red or green?" Nevertheless, the riddle of sense is the origin of science. The physical world illuminated by the light of reason exists by virtue of the question of sensation that besets man. Through it the individual comes to understand his own existence and that of the entire universe. Through it he creates abstract worlds.

8. "Rashba wrote that the reason the blessings were established to address God in both the second person and the third person is that God is both revealed and hidden [the word for 'second person' in Hebrew also means 'present'; the word for 'third person' in Hebrew also means 'hidden'] – revealed in the aspect of His deeds but hidden in the aspect of His Divinity" (Abudraham, *Seder Shaharit shel Hol u-Peirushah, Birkhot ha-Shahar*, s.v. *ve-tzarikh le-nakkot gufo*).

R. Hayyim of Volozhin writes:

> Therefore the members of the Great Assembly established the format of all the blessings in the both the second person and the third person: beginning "Blessed art Thou," which is in the second person, and continuing "Who has sanctified us," which is in the third person, because in the aspect of God's voluntary connection with the worlds, through which we have some small understanding of Him, we speak to Him in the second person, as if He were present, saying, "Blessed art Thou." The worlds themselves require the union of the divine essence with them and the manifold blessings which result from this, and this is the meaning of "King of the universe," another phrase in every blessing; as written in the *Zohar, Raya Mehemna*, II, 42b: "When He goes down to rule over them and He overspreads the creatures, He appears to each one according to his appearance, vision, and imagination, as it is written, 'And through their prophets I am represented in similitudes' (Hosea 12:11)." "The One who commands us and sanctifies us with His essence is the Infinite One, May He Be Blessed, alone, who is the most hidden of all that is hidden. That is why they established the latter part of every blessing in the

third person: "Who has sanctified us with His commandments and commanded us" (*Nefesh ha-Hayyim* 2:3).

9. The tragic failure of the mind's ambition to grasp reality is described in the *Zohar*, in the introduction to the commentary on Genesis (*Zohar* I, 1a–1b):

> R. Eleazar opened his discourse with the text: "Lift high your eyes and see: who created these?" (Isa. 40:26). "Lift up your eyes on high": to which place? To that place to which all eyes are turned, to wit, *Petah Einayaim* ("eye-opener"; Gen. 38:14). By doing so, you will know that it is the mysterious Ancient One, whose essence can be sought, but not found, that created these: to wit, *Mi* (Who?) [*Binah*], that same who is called "from (Heb. *mi*) the extremity of heaven on high" (Deut. 4:32), because everything is in His power, and because He is ever to be sought, though mysterious and un-revealable, since further we cannot enquire.
>
> That extremity of heaven is called *Mi*, but there is another lower extremity which is called *Mah* (What?). The difference between the two is this. The first is the real subject of enquiry, but after a man by means of enquiry and reflection has reached the utmost limit of knowledge, he stops at *Mah* (What?), as if to say, what knowest thou? What have thy searchings achieved? Everything is as baffling as at the beginning.

Here the *Zohar* is discussing the question that is cast between "What" and "Who." Man grasps everything from the perspective of "what are these?" but he does not have the capacity to reveal the *Who*. The *Who* in and of itself remains obscure.

10. All the Jewish sages agree that a religious person must begin with the divine revelation, because it is impossible to strive to know God without faith and tradition. But they were divided in their opinions about the mutual links between these two domains – the revelational and the rational. R. Sa'adyah Gaon and Maimonides, by stressing the continuity between the two domains – where the rational ends, the revelational begins – ignored the distinctive marks that give them their unique character and different patterns. In contrast, R. Bahya and R. Judah Halevi (although they did not deny the continuity principle) looked at

the revelation mainly from a normative standpoint and devoted their appropriate inquiries to clarifying the uniqueness and originality of these two experiences. The authors of *Beliefs and Opinions* [Saʻadyah] and *Guide of the Perplexed* [Maimonides] believe that, even though man – who is imprisoned in the darkness of the sensible world, lives a short life full of vexation, and is subjugated to his senses – cannot encompass the revelational content with his intellect, such a capacity is not inconceivable *ab initio*. Our forefather Abraham recognized his Creator out of his own capacity before He revealed Himself to him (Laws of Idolatry, chap. 1). From the mountaintop of abstract cognition, pure reason which "has torn away all the intervening curtains" can peer into the transcendent realm.

In *The Book of Beliefs and Opinions* (Introduction, 6), R. Saʻadyah writes:

> The Sages tried to prevent us from brushing aside the prophetic Scriptures and relying on our own personal judgment in our specu-lations about the origin of space and time. For one who speculates [philosophizes] after this manner may sometimes find the truth and sometimes go astray; until he has found the truth, he will be without religion; and even if he finds the truth of religion and clings to it, he can never be sure that he will not depart from it should doubts arise in his mind and weaken his belief.… God knew in His wisdom that the final propositions which result from the labor of specula-tion [philosophy] can only be attained in a certain measure of time. Had He, therefore, made us depend on speculation for religious knowledge, we should have existed without religion for some time until the work of speculation was completed and our labor had come to an end. Perhaps many people would never have completed the work because of their inability and never have finished their labor because of their lack of patience; or doubts may have come upon them, and confused and bewildered their minds. From all these troubles God (may He be exalted and glorified) saved us quickly by sending us His Messenger, announcing Him through the Tradition, and allowing us to see with our own eyes signs in support of it and proofs which cannot be assailed by doubts.… He commanded us to inquire patiently until the truth of Tradition was brought out by speculation…

Saʿadyah adds that there is a special divine promise that anyone who strives with his intellect for the treasures of prophecy will reap the rewards of his cognitive labor:

> He has furthermore informed us, however, that if we engage in speculation and diligent research, inquiry will produce for us in each instance the complete truth, tallying with His announcement to us by the speech of His prophets. Besides that He has given us the assurance that heretics will never be in a position to offer a proof against our religion, nor the skeptics to produce an argument against our creed (Ibid.).

These sharp and thoroughly lucid remarks attest to R. Saʿadyah's belief in the identity of the rational and the revelational. In the third part [of *The Book of Beliefs and Opinions*], "Commandment and Prohibition," he says that the revelational vision appears for two reasons: (1) to inform us of commandments which cannot be deduced through reason; (2) to let us know the exact measures and forms of man's divinely prescribed obligation in fulfilling various commandments. (The latter is the favorite explanation of Jewish luminaries, and the echoes of the halakhic voice emerge from it. R. Bahya and R. Judah Halevi also utilized this explanation.)

Maimonides held to the same train of thought:

> ...if we never in any way acquired an opinion by following traditional authority and were not correctly conducted toward something by means of parables, but were obliged to achieve a perfect representation by means of essential definitions and by pronouncing true only that which is meant to be pronounced true in virtue of demonstration – which would be impossible except after the above-mentioned preliminary studies – this state of affairs would lead to all people dying without having known whether there is a Deity for the world or whether there is not, much less whether a proposition should be affirmed with regard to Him or a defect denied. Nobody would ever be saved from this perdition except "one of a city or two of a family" (Jer. 3:14) (*Guide of the Perplexed* 1:34).

And in *The Epistle to Yemen*:

> Ever since the time of Revelation, every despot or slave who has attained to power, be he violent or ignoble, has made it his first aim and

his final purpose to destroy our Law, and to vitiate our religion, by means of the sword, by violence, or by brute force, such as Amalek, Sisera, Sennacherib, Nebuchadnezzar, Titus, Hadrian, may their bones be ground to dust, and others like them. This is one of the two classes which attempt to foil the divine will.

The second class consists of the most intelligent and educated among the nations, such as the Syrians, the Persians, and the Greeks. They too endeavor to demolish our Law and to vitiate it by means of arguments which they invent, and by means of controversies which they institute. They seek to render the Law ineffectual and to wipe out every trace thereof by means of their polemical writings, just as the despots plan to do with the sword. But neither the one nor the other shall succeed. We possess the divine assurance given to Isaiah concerning any tyrant who may wish to undermine our Law and to annihilate it by weapons of war, that the Lord will demolish them so that they will have no effect. This is only a metaphorical way of saying that his efforts will be of no avail, and that he will not accomplish his purpose. In like manner, whenever a disputant shall attempt to demonstrate the falsity of our Law, the Lord will shatter his arguments and prove them absurd, untenable, and ineffective. This divine promise is contained in the following verse, "No weapon that is formed against you shall prosper; and every tongue that shall rise against you in judgment you shall condemn" (Isa. 54:17).

Words of this sort, suffused with exalted love for the community of Israel and its Torah, and which Maimonides wrote to the Jewish exiles in Yemen, forcefully accentuate the principle of parallelism in our great master's view: the possibility of attaining prophecy is promised to us by the Holy One, Blessed Be He, along with the eternity of the Jewish nation and its Torah.

Although R. Bahya also relied on R. Sa'adyah's reasons, he was aware of the distinct and unique characteristics of each of the two basic experiences in religion: the experience of faith and the experience of rational religiosity (in his words, Torah enlightenment and intellectual enlightenment). The former is "a surrender of anxiety and anticipation" which occurs out of necessity and force, while the latter is "the surrender of obligation" (that is, an experience flowing from one's free intellectual and moral consciousness, which R. Bahya calls "the obligation of gratitude").

> It is right to aggrandize and exalt the one to whom he submits....
> [This] is not founded on hope and anxiety, but on wisdom and
> knowledge of what service a person owes to the Creator. Second,
> service of God rooted in the Torah is only rendered as the result of
> hope of reward or anxiety regarding punishment; but the service
> rooted in the understanding comes from willingness of the soul
> and its desire to strive with all its might to serve its God for His own
> sake, as a result of knowledge and comprehension. For the soul will
> freely give all it has, provided it is convinced that what it gives is
> exceeded in value by what it receives in exchange, and this [boon]
> is that God is pleased with it (*Duties of the Heart*, Gate of Divine
> Worship, chap. 3).

The Hasid of Cordova [Bahya], who was greater than all the scho-
lastic and modern philosophers, sensed with a wondrous intuition the
distinct characteristics of the revelational and intellectual experiences
of the man of God, seeing the entire world shining with the rays of the
hidden light. The former experience is an expression of the Infinite
revealing itself to man. The flesh-and-blood individual is swept away
in a supranatural storm within which is revealed the Heavenly experience, crystallized in a feeling of compulsion and fear, as well as in the
form of a decisive, powerful imperative hewed out of the concealed
and separated eternity. The latter experience is one in which the joy of
free creativity bubbles up. It flows from the generosity of the heart and
the freedom of the conquering spirit. Man seeks the Eternal in order
to deepen and broaden his experience. It is characteristic of R. Bahya's
view that the fundamental principle of reward and punishment is connected with the revelational experience of the Infinite, which hides
itself, separates itself, and yet subdues man and forces him to do His
will. Spontaneous religious experience occurs without the intention of
obtaining a reward and has no need of the promise of reward or the
threat of punishment.

On the issue of spiritual evolution as well, the Judge of Cordova
knows that while revelational faith is entirely restricted to a special
realm that precludes change or transformation, intellectual religiosity
is subject to trends that fluctuate during the course of history and the
fate of intellectual developments. It sets aside a place for constant expansion and deepening and continuous movement:

Fifth, the commandments of the Torah are finite; they are a known number, 613 precepts. But the duties imposed by the intellect are almost infinite, for a person increases his knowledge of them daily; and the more his cognition develops and the more he comprehends God's beneficence, His power, and His sovereignty, the more will he surrender and humble himself before Him. Thus you find that David, peace be on him, beseeched God to arouse him to the knowledge of these duties and remove the curtain of folly from his eyes; as it is said, "Open my eyes that I may behold wondrous things out of Your Law" (Ps. 119:18); "Teach me, O Lord, the way of Your statutes" (Ps. 119:33); "Lead me in the path of Your commandments" (Ps. 119:35); "Incline my heart to Your testimonies" (Ps. 119:36). Furthermore it is said, "To all perfection have I seen an end; but Your commandment is exceedingly broad" (Ps. 119:96); that is to say, our obligation of service to You for Your continual benefits to us is without limit, because there is no limit to the variety of Your bounties to us. (Ibid.)

The more scientific knowledge grows, the deeper the questions man will ask, and the more his longing for the living God will intensify.

This description clearly is relevant only to the first state, in which the intellectual experience is distinguished from the revelational experience. We have not yet discussed the second and third states, but R. Bahya deals with them as well in his examination of prophecy and its purpose:

Fifth, the stimulus of the Torah is a preparation for, and introduction to, that of the intellect, the reason being that a man in his youth needs training and guidance.... Thus, the instruction of the Torah turns about hope and fear – the poles of its axis. Whoever does not fall short in fulfilling the obligations of this service belongs to the class of the truly pious and is worthy of reward in this world and in the next. But one who rises from this stage to the service of God, induced by reason, reaches the degree of the prophets and the elect of the Supreme – the saints (Ibid.).

Likewise the Judge [R. Bahya] insisted upon the secret of revelation as an exoteric vision available to everyone, whereas the noetic striving for God is a private, esoteric act.

Third, the intellectual urge cannot comprehend equally all who are under the obligation of service, because some human beings are of limited intelligence, while some are superior in apprehension. But the urge of the Torah applies equally to all who have reached the status subjecting them to this service, even though they vary in their understanding of it…. It sometimes also happens that a person falls short in some duties and excels in others. The intellectual stimulus varies in different individuals in accordance with their capacity of apprehension. But the urge of the Torah is not subject to variation. Its obligation is the same for the child, the youth, one advanced in years and the old man, the wise and the foolish…. And so Scripture says in regard to the comprehensive character of the instruction of the Torah for all people, "Gather the people together, men and women, and children, and the stranger that is within your gate, that they may hear and that they may learn and fear the Lord your God" (Deut. 31:12). Further it is said, "You shall read this law before all Israel in their hearing" (Deut. 31:11) (Ibid.).

The exoteric aspect of Torah enlightenment, however, refers only to the actual objective action, not the subjective experience. Understanding the actions belongs to the individual.

"His recompense here on earth is joy in the sweetness of the service of the Lord, as the prophet said, 'Your words were found, and I ate them; and Your word was to me the joy and rejoicing of my heart, for I am called by Your name' (Jer. 15:16)" (Ibid.). The second and third states are expressly described in this section. Joy and sweetness succeed dimness and longing, and Jeremiah says, "Your words were found," that is to say: I sought them, but I did not find them, I had no reward for all my cognitive toil, but suddenly they were revealed to me, without any expectation or hope; yet in all this I am dedicated to God and my eyes look toward God. "I ate them," and I derived complete satisfaction from them, they became a source of salvation and comfort for me; my heart, saturated with happiness and joy, longs for You.

The prophet waits for the revelation of the *Shekhinah* because he knows that the entire world is nothing but the reflection of eternity. The secret of freedom shines forth brilliantly out of the dimness of compulsion that cloaks the giving of the Law. The individual who is compelled by the revelation to perform specific acts can attain the consciousness of freedom by identifying with the command and transforming the compulsion into a constitution of freedom that is nurtured by God's hidden uniqueness.

To be sure, in the section called "Love of God," Bahya knows how to write about the individual's desire for God, which is mixed with awe at first, yet ends in pure love filled with unceasing yearning for the living God without any fear or retreat.

> What is Love of God? It is the soul's yearning for the Creator, and turning to Him of her own accord, so that she can cleave to His supernal light.... Then she will withdraw from the secular world and its pleasures and will despise physical bodies and all their lusts. Her eyes will be opened and her vision will be cleared of the cloud of ignorance of God and His Law. She will distinguish truth from falsehood, and a clearer conception of the truth concerning her Creator and Guide will be revealed to her. And when she realizes the Almighty's infinite power and essential sublimity, she will bow down and prostrate herself before Him in fear, dread, and awe, inspired by His power and greatness [the first state], and will not depart from this attitude until the Creator, exalted be He, reassures her and quiets her fear and dread. Then her thirst will be assuaged [by drinking deep] out of the cup of love of God, and she will enjoy the bliss of being alone with God, devoting her heart wholly to Him, loving Him, putting her trust in Him and yearning for Him (*Duties of the Heart*, Gate of Love of God 1).

Love begins with awe and fear of God, longing and retreat; it concludes with rushing toward and clinging to Him, enflamed with holy fire.

11. R. Judah Halevi almost completely displaced the element of repulsive fear from divine revelation, concentrating it entirely in the second state (see note 10). He puts his main emphasis on the palpability of the vision, with its enrapturing tapestry of sights. The starting point of Halevi's thought is the failure of reason and the intellectual, syllogistic approach in its quest for God. If man seeks God through the activities of abstraction and deduction, then man will never find Him. Man with his prideful mind can reach the Prime Mover, the thought of all thoughts, the One, the supreme good, absolute perfection, and other such similar attributes. Yet he can never reach the living God that "souls yearn for" (*Kuzari* IV:16). Multitudes of concepts, abstractions, and logical analyses

separate the living God from one who engages in profound and intensive study. The rationalist will never reach the desired destination – [to be in the] bosom of the *Shekhinah*. The philosopher does not long for God from a raging soul, sick with love and driven by yearning, burning with a holy flame, but rather out of cognitive curiosity. He strides only toward a noetic goal:

> The [followers of a religion]...seek God not only for the sake of knowing Him, but also for other benefits which they derive therefrom. The philosopher, however, only seeks Him that he may be able to describe Him accurately in detail, as he would describe the earth, explaining that it is in the center of the great sphere, but not in that of the zodiac, and so on (*Kuzari* IV:13).

In other words, cognitive man's attempt to come closer to God is not rooted in an imperative revelational connection, in longings for the redemption of personal reality and for the saving of the world as a whole. He is wrapped in contemplative tranquility; his goal is ontocentric, not theocentric. He wants to grasp the essence of reality, and therefore he strives toward its source.

The God of Abraham – the God of prophecy – reveals Himself to man in virtue of the latter's human singularity and primal image (*tzelem*) [the image of God]. The link between God and man is very intimate and is manifested in unmediated contact. The divine revelation emerges from a point beyond generality; it is entirely dedicated to the prophet's individuality and personality, and it issues charges and promises about the improvement of his ways and his deeds. God speaks to man as one person speaks to another. The prophet sees a vision of God.

> None of them applies a distinct proper name to God, except he who hears His address, command, or prohibition, approval for obedience, and reproof for disobedience. He bestows some name on Him as an appellation for Him who spoke to him, and he is convinced that He is the Creator of the world from naught. The first man would never have known Him if He had not addressed, rewarded, and punished him.... This gave him the conviction that this was the Creator of the world, whom he designated by words and attributes, and styled "Lord." Without this he would have been left with the name Elokim (*Kuzari* IV:3)...And because He established a connection with man,

the name Elokim was altered after the creation into A-donai Elokim. This the Sages express in the words "A full name over a full universe" (*Gen. Rabbah* 13:3). The world was completed only with the creation of man, who forms the heart of all that was created before him (*Kuzari* IV:15).

In Halevi's opinion, the divine name Elokim denotes the cosmic revelation of God, whereas the Tetragrammaton denotes the prophetic revelation. The divine revelation assumes a sensory wrapping. The prophets, "with their inner eye," see "forms that are appropriate to their nature." The divine emanation is felt by man, and the divine vision becomes a living, permeating sensation. While the intellect abstracts, the prophet's eye beholds a vision of God, and he feels Him with all his senses.

The prophet feels God. His entire body and senses are caught up in a wondrous vision brimming with life content, a life raging with intensity and force. In place of the shadows of abstract ideas, the "piercing light" and the infinite "glory" find their way in.

Halevi writes about a transcendent, supranatural, divine existence which the prophet encounters and perceives. He tries to ground religion particularly in actual experience which accouters itself in the variegated qualitative sense-contents that fill man's life.

> In this way, the prophets' images picture God's greatness, power, loving-kindness, omniscience, life, eternity, government, and independence, the dependence of everything on Him, His unity and holiness, and in one sudden flash stands revealed this grand and majestic figure with its splendor, its characteristics, the instruments that typify power, such as the uplifted hand, the unsheathed sword, fire, wind, thunder and lightning, which obey His behest, the word that goes forth.... He raises the lowly, humbles the mighty, and holds out His hand to the repentant.... He is wroth with the wicked... while before Him "thousands upon thousands minister unto Him" (Dan. 7:10). Such are the visions that the prophet sees in one moment. Thus fear and love come to him naturally, and remain in his heart for the whole of his life. He even yearns for the vision again and again (*Kuzari* IV:5).

Although the term "fear" is mentioned here only in passing, it hints at the feeling of fear that besets man, as we explained in our description of the first experience. Nevertheless, a reader who studies the text intensively will sense that Halevi's description of the prophetic vision is analogous not to the experience of panic-ridden anxiety and recoil discussed by R. Bahya and Maimonides, but rather to the experience of love suffused with awe of the beloved that leads to yearning. See note 2 for Maimonides' view.

12. This entire matter is explained in R. Isaac Luria's doctrine of *tzimtzum* [constriction]. In this view, God "constricted" His glory in order to create the world, leaving an open, empty "space in the middle" – that is, the act of creation is composed of separation and advance. God separated Himself from the world when He had the idea of creating it, and this separation is the beginning of the act of creation, since the world cannot exist in the bosom of the Holy One, Blessed Be He, as His infinite being precludes any other existence. On the other hand, God is the one who brings being into existence, and it cannot continue to exist without depending on Him. The absence of His glory is identical with total nothingness. Complete separation negates the existent even before it is created. Therefore, His glory radiated both an external light (which surrounds the entire world) and an internal light (which fills the entire world), and this radiance is embodied in everything that exists in the world.

> Insofar as the *Ein Sof* [Infinite] initially fills the space of all the worlds which He created thereafter, there was then no empty space; and the *Ein Sof* had to constrict His Presence and His light, leaving an empty place, in order to emanate into the worlds. This constriction, however, was not from the *Ein Sof*'s perspective, but rather through intermediation. And since the *Ein Sof* emanated forth and left a space for Creation within the worlds, He saw that if His light were to remain constricted when He emanates worlds into that empty space, without any penetration of the *Ein Sof*'s light into their inner being, but rather illuminates that which is external to them in the sense of a light that surrounds them from outside.... They all possess an inner light within the vessel, and the outer light surrounds everything else that is inside it...(R. Hayyim Vital, *Neveh She'arim* 1:1).
>
> And this is what we ask...that in all of them there be the extension and revelation of the light of the *Ein Sof*, Blessed Be His Great Name, so that Being not be annulled to Nothingness. For because of

the illumination of Being (*Havayah*) that brings about existence in the progression of worlds, Nothingness was turned into Being. And whatever devolves and descends downward became more existent until the literally separate worlds came into being. But in the revelation of the light of the *Ein Sof* that is above progression, the worlds will be annulled from Being to Nothingness (R. Schneur Zalman of Lyadi, *Likkutei Torah* [Vilna, 1928]), *Shelah* 48:3b).

The story told by R. Nahman of Bratzlav about the heart of the world pursuing the spring reflects this idea. [See the story "The Seven Beggars," in *Sippurei Ma'asiyyot* #13, the third day. "Were the Heart to cease looking at the Spring, it would die, because its whole existence comes from the Spring. As long as it stands at a distance, it can see the summit of the mountain and the Spring. But as soon as it gets close to the mountain, it loses sight of the summit and therefore of the Spring; and it starts to die, God forbid."]

Consider Rashi's commentary on the song sung by the Israelites at the Red Sea, "*Ozzi ve-zimrat Y-H, vayehi li li-yeshuah*" (Ex. 15:2):

> Therefore I say…*ozzi* is a noun…. The praise, therefore, [proclaimed in these words] is this: the *ozzi* and the *zimrat* of God, this to me was a salvation. The word *zimrat* is a noun in the construct state to the word which expresses the divine name…. The expression *ve-zimrat* has the meaning [of the root which we find in] "you shall not prune" (Lev. 25:4), "the cutting down of the terrible ones" (Isa. 25:5), [both of which] have the meaning "lopping off" and "cutting down." [Thus the verse signifies:] The strength and vengeance of our God has become to us a salvation.

That is, God reveals Himself both as *ozzi*, "refuge and shield," and as *zimrat*, "annihilation and destruction." Both of these attributes saved the Israelites at the Red Sea. Likewise, Rashi was precise in his commentary on a later verse in the same song, "Your right hand, O God, is glorious in power; Your right hand, O God, has dashed in pieces the enemy" (Ex. 15:6): "But it seems to me that the self-same right hand [that saves Israel] itself dashes the enemy in pieces, something which is impossible for man – to do two actions with one hand." The marvelous idea is expressed once again. See also Ibn Ezra's commentary on Ex. 3:14.

See the *Yalkut* on the last verse of Psalms:

"Every soul will praise the Lord." R. Hiyya bar Abba of Jaffa said: "The soul in man is always ascending and descending and trying to leave him, so how does it stay within the body? Since God's glory fills the world, when the soul tries to leave the body it sees its Creator and retreats. Therefore every soul, whenever it ascends and descends, will praise God for the miracles He performs for it."

The act of running "back and forth" finds explicit expression in this quotation. See also *Zohar, Raya Mehemna* III, 229b; *Etz Hayyim, Sha'ar Kissei ha-Kavod*, chap. 7; *Likkutei Torah, Parashat Hukkat*, 3:21b.

Maimonides – who placed the world's yearning for its Creator in the center of the Jewish perspective, not only as a moral ideal embodied in man's longing to cleave to His God, but also as a dynamic metaphysical force that engenders the cosmic motion, since the world is an individuum, a great man, a *macro-anthropos* – also insisted that awe is an inseparable part of love. Advance and recoil, bold yearning and urgent retreat blend together into an intense paradoxical emotion that attacks one who is laden with the awe of God; love melds with awe.

This God, honored and revered – it is our duty to love Him and fear Him, as it is said, "You shall love the Lord your God" (Deut. 6:5), and it is further said, "You shall revere the Lord your God" (ibid. 6:13). And what is the way to love Him? When a person contemplates His great and wondrous works and creatures, and from them sees His wisdom, incomparable and infinite, he will straightaway love Him, praise Him, glorify Him, and long with an exceeding longing to know His great name, as David said, "My soul thirsts for God, for the living God" (Ps. 42:3). And when he ponders these matters, he will recoil frightened, and realize that he is a small creature, lowly and obscure, endowed with slight and slender intelligence, standing in the presence of Him who is perfect in knowledge. And so David said: "When I consider Your heavens, the work of Your fingers – what is man that You are mindful of him" (Ps. 8:4–5) (Laws of the Foundations of the Torah 2:2).

When one reflects on these things, and comes to know all created beings…and sees His wisdom in all created things – His love for God will increase, his soul will thirst, his very flesh will yearn to love God. He will be filled with fear and trembling because of his lowly condition, his poverty, his insignificance…He will then realize that he is a vessel full of shame and dishonor, empty and deficient (Laws of the Foundations of the Torah 4:12).

Encounter conjoins with retreat, longing with awe. Man charges forward and retreats, yearns yet fears, beholds the eternal vision and hides his face. The awe discussed in works of theology and homiletics is essentially fear of the loss of independent existence, which emerges from the realization of the longing for preservation of selfhood. There is good reason for Maimonides to use two different attributes for God – *nikhbad* [venerated] and *nora* [awesome] – because the former denotes the positive element, which establishes and maintains the world, while the second refers to the negative element, which abrogates the world. Both of these are important elements of this antithetic complex of love and awe. It seems to me that Maimonides obtained this idea from the Judge of Cordova's [R. Bahya's] work:

> What is love of God? It is the soul's yearning for the Creator, and turning to Him of her own accord, so that she shall cleave to His supernal light.... And when she realizes the Almighty's infinite power and essential sublimity, she will bow down and prostrate herself before Him in fear, dread and awe, inspired by His power and greatness (*Duties of the Heart*, Gate of Love of God, Ch. 1).

This idea is also expressed by Nahmanides:

> The meaning of "You shall fear the Lord your God" is that after commanding love [of God], it [the Torah] mentions fear of Him, so that one will not sin and be punished. "And you shall serve Him to do what He has commanded you" – like a slave who fulfills the commands of his master (Commentary to Deut. 6:13).

Nahmanides stressed the value of fear as well as of total subjugation. Even in the context of the commandment to love God, the Torah stressed this approach.

13. Actually, the expression *pahad Elokim* [fear of God] is generally found in the Scriptures in a negative sense, as dread that paralyzes man's vitality: "And the terror of God was upon the cities" (Gen. 35:5) [ensuring the safety of Jacob and his family]; "Terror and dread will descend

upon them" (Ex. 15:16) [in reference to the other nations' reactions to the drowning of the Egyptians in the Red Sea]; "Sinners will be afraid in Zion" (Isa. 33:14). The primary commandment is *yir'ah* [reverence or awe of God]: "You shall revere your God" (Deut. 6:13, 10:20); "but only to revere God" (Deut. 10:12).

There are also, however, some expressions in the Scriptures that emphasize the positive value of fear (*pahad*): God is described as "*pahad Yitzhak*," the One whom Isaac feared; King Solomon says, "Happy is one who is always afraid" (Prov. 28:14). See *Berakhot* 60a, the section beginning "That disciple..." Another such expression is found in Psalms 36:2: "The speech of sin to the sinner is clear to me: There is no fear of God holding his attention." Apparently, fear is the first step with which humankind begins. The goal is awe of God. It is impossible for this awe to develop, however, if it is not preceded by fear. Man's first reaction to being subdued by God is the emotion of fear or dread. Even the complete man of the Torah, such as the *hasid* [very pious person], cannot free himself of the basic feeling of fear in the religious experience. This fear nettles the depths of his being. Awe is merely the sublimation and redemption of this fear.

> Anyone who fears Heaven seeks that which is hidden...and has no anxiety, as it is written, "Sinners were fearful in Zion" (Is. 33:14). He fears sin, but he is not anxious, because the *Shekhinah* acts as armor for him and protects him (*Massekhet Atzilut*, sec. 1; see also the commentary *Ginzei Meromim* by R. Isaac Haver ad loc.).

R. Joseph Gikatilla stated:

> After we have taught you these great principles, we must repeat the secret of the attribute of the divine name Elokim, which is the attribute of fear and of divine judgment, the attribute ascribed to Isaac.... Now I have taught you that even though the attribute ascribed to Isaac is fear, his intention was to benefit the Israelite people.... And if not for fear of the judgment of Gehinnom, many righteous people would be sinners, so there is a great benefit to the attribute of fear ascribed to Isaac, because people's fear of the judgment of Gehinnom makes them beware of sins that might lead to it. And this is the secret of the fear of Isaac, about which it is written, "Happy is the man who is always afraid" (*Sha'arei Orah*, v).

14. R. Isaiah Halevi Ish-Horowitz, the author of the *Shelah*, or *Shenei Luhot ha-Berit* [The Two Tablets of the Covenant], distinguished external fear and love (fear of punishment and love of reward) from inner awe and love (fear of the exalted, whose source is the sense of shame, and love rooted in gratitude). The latter sort of love is active, filled with desire and devotion. This Kabbalist stressed the element of gratitude, following the view of R. Bahya, rather than the element of wisdom and knowledge, as is the view of Maimonides. The *Shelah* is aware, however, of a level higher than all of these:

> Fear and love of the innermost sort come to perfect the King with the honor of the names Y-H-W-H and Elokim. Fear comes to complete the secret of the union of *Tiferet* [Glory] and *Malkhut* [Kingship]. Hidden and great love comes to complete the union of *Hokhmah* [Wisdom] and *Binah* [Understanding]. The highest aim is the cleaving of creation to its Creator and the mystical unification of the great and awesome name (*Asarah Ma'amarot* [Ten Utterances] 1–2).

The *Sifrei* on Deuteronomy puts it this way:

> "And you shall love the Lord your God" – act out of love (*ahavah*). Scripture distinguished between those who act out of love and those who act out of fear (*yir'ah*).... As it is written, "And you shall fear the Lord your God and worship Him" – there are those who are afraid of others, and when they are burdensome, they leave them. But you must act out of love, and there is no love where there is fear, or fear where there is love, except with relation to God Himself (*Sifrei*, Deut. 32).

This explanation in the *Sifrei*, which insists upon the antithetical nature of love and fear, refers to the love-fear complex. It is impossible to love someone whom one fears. In relation to God, however, even fear (in the first experience) can be combined with love (in the second experience). As we stressed above, even after fear is raised to the level of awe of the exalted, the element of fear does not disappear entirely. It still permeates the depths of the phenomenon.

Maimonides included those who perform the commandments

in order to obtain life in the world-to-come in the category of people who worship God for the sake of a reward. The author of *Shenei Luhot ha-Berit* criticized his view, saying that such people are in the category of those who worship God without expecting a reward. However, Maimonides defined worship out of love as follows:

> The person who worships out of love occupies himself with the study of the Law and the fulfillment of the commandments...impelled by no external motive whatsoever, moved neither by fear of calamity nor by the desire to obtain material benefits – such a person does what is truly right because it is truly right, and ultimately the good comes to him as a result of his conduct (Laws of Repentance 10:2).

Apparently, then, in Maimonides' view there are two distinct relations between those who perform the commandments and the issue of life in the world-to-come. The first relation finds expression in the person who performs the commandments and perceives eternal life as a reward for his doing so, as though eternal life were not a direct metaphysical result of a properly ordered life in accordance with the Torah in this world, but a reward given by God. Such an attitude to eternal life is in the category of "worship in order to obtain a reward." The second attitude is totally different. It conceives of eternal life as a necessary result of a life imbued with Torah in this world. Transcendent existence of an eternal nature actually begins with this – cleaving to God through the achievements of one's intellect, activity, and will. The end result, the eternal good, must necessarily arrive as a logical conclusion that emerges from the assumption. One who worships God out of love performs the commandments and studies the Torah not in order to attain the world-to-come as a reward for his achievements, but as a continuation of his pure and holy life in this world. There is a good reason for our Sages' analogy between the Sabbath and the world-to-come.

The *Sifrei* offers the following commentary in Deuteronomy, *Parashat Ekev* (41): "...lest one say, 'I will study the Torah in order to become rich, in order to be called Rabbi, in order to get a reward in the world-to-come.'" This is the version of the midrashic commentary quoted by Maimonides. Rashi apparently had a version that ended, "in order to receive a reward in this world" (Rashi to Deut. 11:13).

This commentary of *Sifrei* requires study, because someone who studies the Torah in order to glorify himself before other people is regarded as a flatterer, and is not even on the level of those who worship God out of fear of punishment or hope of reward. The punishment and the reward in this sense must come from the Holy One, Blessed Be He. Heaven forbid that this fear or hope should be felt with respect to other people.

The word *yir'ah*, which usually means "awe," is sometimes used in the Talmud to signify "fear"; likewise, the word *ahavah*, which usually means "love," is sometimes used to signify "trust" (*bittahon*). Consider the usage in *Sotah* 22b:

> Abbaye and Rava said to the Tanna: Do not teach: "a *parush* [abstemious person] out of love and a *parush* out of fear [are included in the types of *perushim* who destroy the world]." For R. Judah said in the name of Rav: "One should always engage in the [study of] Torah and [the fulfillment of] the commandments [even if] not for their own sake, because [engagement] not for their own sake will lead to [engagement] for their own sake."

Rashi comments here that, in this case, *ahavah* and *yir'ah* refer to the hope for reward and the fear of punishment. See the commentary of Tosafot, s.v. *le-olam*. Also see the Tosafot commentaries on *Yevamot* 48b, s.v. *she-ein*, and on *Avodah Zarah* 19a, s.v. *al menat*. See also *Rosh Hashanah* 4a.

Also consider the usage in *Sotah* 31a:

> We have learned: R. Meir says: "Job was called 'God-fearing,' and Abraham was called 'God-fearing.' Just as the appellation 'God-fearing' used of Abraham means that he served God out of love, the appellation 'God-fearing' used of Job also means that he worshiped God out of love."... What is the difference between performing the commandments out of love and performing them out of fear? There is a difference, as R. Shim'on ben Eli'ezer says: "One who performs the commandments out of love is greater than one who performs the commandments out of fear."

Cf. Rashi ad loc.:

> These are unlike those who are *parush* [abstemious] out of love or fear, because the latter act out of love of divine reward and fear of

retribution, the maledictions and the punishments, while the former act out of love and awe of God Himself, as His awe is great and is cast upon His creatures.

The contradiction between love and fear emerges from the passages in the Talmud. Yet the conclusion of the passages demonstrates that the highest level is love. There is a progressive movement from love combined with awe to love combined with desire.

15. The tradition of the names of God is a cornerstone of Judaism's exalted worldview. It is as if it were impossible to approach this view without first appreciating the divine light that is hidden in His names. The holy philosophy of the medieval Jewish sages, as well as the esoteric mystical thought of that period, revealed transcendent metaphysical aspects of God's names and distinguished between the affirmative attributes of divine action and the negative attributes of His essence. Excelling in particular in this endeavor was Maimonides, the master of the Halakhah, who applied his powerful spirit to the issue of divine names and cast clear light upon them. In the view of our great teacher, the Tetragrammaton, which is also called the Singular Name or the Explicit Name of God, always appears, according to the Halakhah, as a name denoting God's essence. The Explicit Name is distinct in its essence and unique and determinate in its character. Many *halakhot* were formulated in regard to it. Jewish religious consciousness has bound many crowns of marvelous secrets to each and every ornamental line on its letters, and this revered and awesome Name was crowned with the attribution of fiery flames, bursting the bounds of Creation. The Explicit Name carves out a window to the awesome mystery of the destruction of being via its approach to its source. The simple, sole, unique Infinite, which includes all and negates all, encompasses everything and fills everything ("there is no place that is free of Him"), is revealed in these four arcane letters.

The Explicit Name has a special status in the Halakhah. These are the characteristic laws associated with this name of God:

(1) It may not be uttered outside the Holy Temple; therefore it is always read as A-donai rather than as written.

(2) It may be uttered in the Holy Temple. In the Priestly Blessing, in the High Priest's confession on Yom Kippur, and when selecting the

goat as a sin-offering to God on Yom Kippur, it is an obligation to utter it. In the case of the Priestly Blessing offered in the Temple, the commandment is not fulfilled – so it appears from Maimonides – unless the Explicit Name is uttered (Laws of Prayer and the Priestly Blessing 14:10). But there is some doubt about this, because even though the commandment of uttering the Priestly Blessing in the Temple is not fulfilled without the utterance of the Explicit Name, if the priests uttered the blessing with another name of God, they did at least fulfill the commandment of uttering the Priestly Blessing as performed outside of the Temple confines. With regard to the Yom Kippur confession, [when the High Priest utters the Tetragrammaton three times in each of his three confessions] and [the designation by lottery of the sacrificial goat for the purpose of a sin offering, when the priest selecting the lot] calls out "a sin offering to God!" [pronouncing the Tetragrammaton], we do not know whether failing to pronounce the Explicit Name prevents either commandment from being fulfilled.

(3) The oath uttered by a *sotah* [a woman suspected by her husband of having committed adultery in secret] requires the utterance of the Explicit Name, as explained in the Talmud (*Shevu'ot* 35b).

(4) R. Hanina bar Idi (ibid.) holds that all other oaths require the utterance of the Explicit Name (whenever the Halakhah requires the utterance of a divine name; the medieval authorities differed over the details of the laws of when oaths require the utterance of God's name).

(5) According to R. Abraham ben David (Rabad), based on the Jerusalem Talmud, a person who curses a peer, a ruler, or a judge is not punishable by lashes unless he utters the Explicit Name in his curse. (See *Hassagot ha-Ravad*, Laws of Sanhedrin 26:3; Jerusalem Talmud, *Sanhedrin* 7:8.)

(6) The medieval halakhic commentators all agree that a person who curses God's name is not punishable by death unless he utters the Tetragrammaton as the object of the curse. As regards the name uttered as the medium of the curse, Maimonides claims that the person uttering the curse is punishable even if he used another of the names of God that may not be erased. R. Meir Abulafiah (Ramah) disagrees, claiming that the person is not punishable unless he also used the Tetragrammaton as the subject of the curse. The medieval authorities also differed about the interpretation of the Tetragrammaton – whether it is the name Y-H-W-H, or the name A-donai, or both. (See Maimonides, Laws of

Idolatry 20:7; *Hiddushei ha-Ramah* to *Sanhedrin 56a*, s.v. *matnitin*, and to *60a*, s.v. *piska amar R. Yehoshua ben Karhah*.)

(7) Maimonides tied the holiness of the name Y-H to the fact "that this is a name which is part of the Explicit Name." Apparently the Explicit Name has a special status of imparting sanctity.

The law that E-L is a separate name of God is not based on the fact that it is part of the name Elokim, because these are listed separately among the names of God that may not be erased. However, the fact that Y-H is considered a name that may not be erased, even when it is used as a name of God by itself, is rooted in the Explicit Name. Two laws were stated with regard to the name Y-H: (1) This part of the Explicit Name becomes holy even if the scribe intended to write the entire Tetragrammaton; (2) this part of the Explicit Name becomes holy even when it is written as a separate name.

Yet these two laws actually constitute one unified law. The difference between the status of the letters Tz-V of the divine name Tzeva-ot and the letters Sh-D of the divine name Sh-addai, on the one hand, and the letters E-L of Elokim and Y-H of Y-H-W-H, on the other, is based on the rule that cloaked the latter in the holiness of the divine name and withheld it from the former. The essence of this rule is that part of a divine name does not acquire holiness unless it too is a divine name. However, see R. Hananel on *Shevu'ot* 35a, where he [quotes a variant reading of the Gemara, according to which] the letters A-D of A-donai are also holy (even though they do not constitute a divine name by themselves). He believes that the two sorts of holiness – that of the divine name in and of itself and that of the letters as the beginning of another divine name – are independent.

The revered and awesome Explicit Name is the true, absolute, and sole reality that abrogates the finite independent existence of the world or of man. Only the Name exists; nothing else exists outside of it. The very concept of "outside" is absurd. There is nothing outside the Infinite. He is everything, He is revealed through everything and embraces all things. It is impossible for the world to exist except by participating in God's existence. However, the participation of the finite in the Infinite is patently impossible, because when finitude is conjoined with infinity, the latter nullifies the former.

"Hear, O Israel, the Lord is our God, the Lord is One." This verse firmly sets down the law for the Jewish faith and Halakhah. The existence of God is both absolute unity and absolute singularity. It abrogates the ontic character of finite existence. The Explicit Name, which denotes infinite unitary being, is not declined in any grammatical form that denotes a relation to some other. No other whatsoever exists in its presence or in relation to it. No possessive pronoun is added to the Explicit Name as a suffix, no definite article is prefixed to it, no possessive form links it with anything.

In any possessive phrase, "the x of y," the nominative, the thing possessed, x, is subordinate to the genitive, the possessor, y. Therefore the Tetragrammaton never appears as the first component of a possessive phrase, although it appears as the second component, y, in many places in the Scriptures. In light of this premise we can understand the statement of our sages in *Shevu'ot* 35b that Tzeva-ot constitutes a divine name in and of itself. At first glance this statement is hard to understand. After all, the phrase in the verse is "Y-H-W-H Tzeva-ot" ["the God of hosts"], where Y-H-W-H is the "possessed" and Tzeva-ot is the "possessor." This is the basis of R. Yosei's thesis when he disputes the other sages and says that the word Tzeva-ot may be erased, because it is only a name of Israel, and the words that are holy, namely, Y-H-W-H Tzeva-ot, have the possessive form. The other Sages disagreed with R. Yosei because the divine name cannot be part of a possessive phrase in which it appears in the nominative. Therefore they interpreted the words Y-H-W-H Tzeva-ot as two divine names, meaning "Y-H-W-H, who is Tzeva-ot."

The Explicit Name denotes total separateness, absolute aloneness, a separateness that is greatly admired and inspires awe in all that surrounds it. This divine name, the Explicit Name, is entirely the negation of relations, the abrogation of freedom. When a member of the Jewish people proclaims the unity of the great Name of God in the morning and evening prayers, he attests to the destruction of the reality of the world and the uniqueness of the reality of God as the one and only Existent, such that there is no other being besides Him. God's unity is also His uniqueness, which negates and abolishes the independent existence of creatures. The "All" that considers itself an independent existence reverts to chaos. The congregation of Israel has proclaimed not only the uniqueness of God, but also the dependence of the universe on Him. The Explicit Name is the symbol of this belief – the exalted divine name which bestows on man the plenitude of the world if he is humble and capable of feeling shame and willing to admit his existential dependence on God. He is also the God who is terrifying to brazen, arrogant people who boast and vaunt themselves for their "independent" existence. Such existence is eradicated by God, and the fear of extinction attacks these people.

A *mishnah* in *Yoma* (3:9) states: "And the priests and the people who were standing in the Temple courtyard, when they heard the Explicit Name emerging from the mouth of the High Priest in holiness and purity, would bow down and prostrate themselves and fall on their faces." Now, what is prostrating oneself and falling on one's face, if not eradicating one's independence and nullifying one's existence?

On the other hand, there are divine names that are called "appellations" by the Halakhah. Some of them may be erased, whereas others may not, and the thought of the mystics and other Jewish sages has discovered attributes or affirmative characterizations in them. Elokim, Shaddai, and the like denote a positive connection between the Creator and His creatures. The descriptions of divine action appeared from within God's hidden separate place when He created the world, "when He decided in His simple will [i.e., not made up of parts] to reveal Himself to the world" (cf. *Sefer ha-Ikkarim* 2:22; Shelah, *Haggahot le-Sefer Toledot ha-Adam, bayit* 4:9; *Etz Hayyim, heikhal* 1, *sha'ar* 1, *anaf* 2) when the affirmative aspect of God's regard for the other emerged from the depths of the Infinite. The coming into being of the other and the continuation of its existence through its dependence on God are encoded in the secrets of the divine names and appellations.

The other approaches its Creator, and through this approach participates in absolute reality and lends it a magnificent, distilled existence. When one mentions Elokim [in a prayer or blessing], one must intend that He is the master of all natural forces. That is, the dynamics of the cosmos is revealed through the name of the Hidden God [Elokim]. When we say Sh-addai, we must intend that "He said to the world, *Dai* [i.e., so far and no farther]." In other words, the quantitative-mathematical laws of nature that are embedded in the world are rooted in this divine name. When we utter the name A-donai ["the Lord"], we must mean that we intently view the world as belonging to God, and likewise with each of the divine names and attributes. In short, all the divine names other than the Explicit name attest to the existence of the world and God's positive connection to it, through which the world exists and the creation is renewed every day.

R. Hayyim of Volozhin states:

After we have proclaimed in the first verse of *Shema* that He is only one, simply one, and that there is nothing else at all, and that all the worlds are as if they do not exist at all, and that there is no one else at all but He, and that all the worlds are as if they do not exist at all, how can we praise Him? He is already blessed in the glory of His kingdom over the worlds, since the worlds too exist, and He, may He be blessed, rules over them (*Nefesh ha-Hayyim* 3:2).

The dynamic aspect of the world is symbolized by God's title of King, just as it is by the divine name Elokim. The natural regularity of the cosmic drama inheres in the name. It is impossible to conceive the appellation of King without placing the world within God's authority. The title of King does not apply to the aspect of absolute separateness from the world. Being a king requires the existence of a nation. In the present context, being the King of the world requires the existence of a world which He created for His honor and within which His name is invoked. He sustains His creatures and makes their singular existence possible. The dependence upon the King does not diminish the image of the creation; on the contrary, the creation is refreshed and renewed by its subjugation to the King. The Tetragrammaton eradicates the universe; the other divine names attest that the world exists as God's kingdom, thus requiring it to exist.

The Jewish sages were divided on the question of whether the Explicit Name characterizes God's essence or only His acts. Maimonides and R. Judah Halevi held that this Name denotes God's essence. Most of the Kabbalists, however, held that the Explicit Name is set aside for God's cloaking Himself in the emanations through His acts.

Halevi expressed his view as follows:

Said the Rabbi: All the names of God, save the Tetragrammaton, are predicates and relative attributive descriptions, derived from the way His creatures are affected by His decrees and measures.... All attributes (excepting the Tetragrammaton) are divided into three classes (*Kuzari* II:2).

Maimonides put it this way in *Guide of the Perplexed* (1:61):

> All the names of God, may He be exalted, that are to be found in any
> of the books derive from actions. There is nothing secret in this mat-
> ter. The only exception is one name, the Tetragrammaton. This is the
> name of God, may He be exalted, that has been originated without
> any derivation, and for this reason it is called the Explicit Name. This
> means that this name signifies His essence, may He be exalted, a sig-
> nification that is distinct and unequivocal [having only one meaning].
> On the other hand, all the other great names signify in an equivocal
> way, being derived from terms signifying actions the like of which...
> exist as our own actions.... Scripture promises that an apprehension
> that will put an end to [the] delusion [that God has many attributes]
> will come to men. Thus it says: "On that day shall the Lord be one
> and His name one" (Zech. 14:9), which means that in the same way as
> He is one, He will be invoked at that time by one name only, by that
> which is indicative only of the essence and is not derivative.

The *Zohar*, however, as we emphasized above, as well as the
Kabbalists who followed its view, believes that the Infinite cannot be
grasped even with the Explicit Name. "It is forbidden to one who apprehends Him as He is before Creation to picture Him under any form
or shape whatsoever, not even by His letters *He, Vav,* and *Yod,* nor by
the whole of His Holy Name, nor by any letter or sign whatsoever"
(*Zohar* II, 42b).

R. Hayyim Vital as well, in *Etz Hayyim* [*Tree of Life*], writes that
the supernal light which is supremely high, without any limit, is called
the Infinite, and its name proves that it cannot be grasped in thought or
imagination in any way whatsoever, being abstract and separated from
all thought (*Sha'ar ha-Kelalim,* chap. 1).

The Vilna Gaon writes, *contra* Maimonides:

> Know that the Infinite, may He be blessed, cannot be thought of at
> all, because it is forbidden to include within Him even the necessity
> of existence. Even the first sphere is called "nothing"; the second is
> called "existence"(*Likkutei ha-Gra, Sifra di-Tzeniy'uta,* 11).

16. The idea that the Creation of the world was a moral act, and that
man must try to imitate God by devoting himself to acts of creativity,

is the foundation of Maimonides' theory of the attributes of action. It is permitted to use attributes that describe the works of the Creator, with which He created the world and continues to govern it, since these are all moral acts – attributes that require man to adapt his actions to them. Prophecy, which revealed God's acts to humans, sees the entire world as the embodiment of the Hidden Intellect within the Supreme Will, as the uncovering of the divine apprehension-volition, which is totally moral and purposeful. This is the source of the moral lawfulness in the world. God provided Moses with knowledge of the entire world through the enlightenment of the thirteen divine attributes, which are the foundations of prophetic morality.

Maimonides expressed this as follows:

> Know that the master of those who know, Moses our Teacher, peace be on him, made two requests and received an answer to both of them. One request consisted in his asking Him, may He be exalted, to let him know His essence and true reality. The second request, which he put first, was that He let him know His attributes.... His request regarding knowledge of [God's] attributes is conveyed in his saying: "Show me now Your ways, that I may know You" (Ex. 33:13).... Then he asked for the apprehension of His essence, may He be exalted. This is what he means when he says, "Show me, I pray, Your glory" (Ex. 33:20); whereupon he received a [favorable] answer with regard to what he had asked for first, namely, "Show me Your ways." For he was told: "I will make all My goodness pass before you" (Ex. 33:19). The phrase "All my goodness" alludes to the display to him of all existing things.... This notion is indicated when it says, "He is trusted in all My house" (Num. 12:7); that is, he has grasped the existence of all My world with a true and firmly established understanding.... Scripture restricts itself to mentioning only the "thirteen characteristics," although [Moses] apprehended "all his goodness" – I mean to say, His actions – because these are the actions proceeding from Him, may He be exalted, in respect of giving existence to people and governing them. This was [Moses'] ultimate object in his demand, the conclusion of what he says being: "That I may know You, to the end that I may find grace in Your sight, and consider that this nation is Your people" (Ex. 33:13), that is, a people for the governance of which I need to perform actions that I must seek to make similar to Your actions in governing them.... It behooves the governor of a

city, if he is a prophet, to acquire similarity to these attributes, so that his actions may proceed from him in accordance with a determined measure and in accordance with the deserts of the people affected by them…for the utmost virtue of man is to become like unto Him, may He be exalted, as far as he is able; which means that we should make our actions like unto His (*Guide of the Perplexed* 1:54).

17. Ibn Gikatilla writes:

And that which our Sages inquired [*Ketubbot* 11b]: "Is it possible for a human being to cleave to the *Shekhinah*?" is all true…and you should know and believe that there is a matter inherent in the secret of the form of the purity of the bodily organs, enabling human beings to cleave to the *Shekhinah*…. This is the fire with which those who cleave to the *Shekhinah* indulge themselves with a pure soul that is called the divine candle. From it the candle of the soul is lit, and it cleaves to it and desires it…(*Sha'arei Orah*, 1).

Nahmanides stated toward the end of his commentary on *Parashat Ekev*:

It is possible that cleaving to God includes the idea that you should always be thinking of God and His love, that your thoughts should never depart from Him. And perhaps people who have this good quality are such that their souls are connected with the source of life even while they are alive, because they themselves are the dwelling-place of the *Shekhinah*, as hinted at by the author of the *Kuzari* (commentary to Deut. 11:22).

R. Judah Halevi's teaching is founded upon the aspiration to cleave to God. The idea of the "divine faculty" that becomes joined to the prophet expresses a metaphysical cleaving to God. Such cleaving can occur on the individual level (the prophet) or the national level (the congregation of Israel). Historical periods encompass the embodiment of the cleaving of the divine faculty to the Jewish people.

Maimonides developed the idea of man's spiritual ascent, that is, cleaving to God in affection and trembling. The basic principles of the Jewish religion – prophecy, divine providence, and the continued existence of the soul after death – are bound up with man's cleaving to God. But while Halevi based man's cleaving to God on an emotional and moral foundation, Maimonides spoke in praise of an intellectual and moral activity. The vision of the Song of Songs is total cleaving to God.

Maimonides' distinction with regard to the permanence of the holiness imparted to *Eretz Yisrael* by Joshua and by Ezra is well known. The first sanctification, imparted to *Eretz Yisrael* by [Joshua's] conquest of the land, was only temporary, lasting as long as the Israelite nation actually lived there. The second sanctification, imparted to the land by Jewish settlement there, is obtained in perpetuity and not abrogated by the Exile. The two sorts of sanctification derive from two different biblical verses. The sanctification imparted by conquest is derived from the verse at the end of *Parashat Ekev* (Deut. 11:24): "Every spot on which your foot treads I have given to you." As explained by Maimonides (Laws of Terumot 1:2), this verse refers to the sanctity imparted to *Eretz Yisrael* through its conquest by the Israelite nation. The sanctity imparted by Ezra is based on the verse in *Parashat Nitzavim*: "And He will benefit you more and make you more numerous than your ancestors" (Deut. 30:5). This verse refers to the later conquest, which was based on a new element: the sanctification of the land through settlement without an act of conquest and aggression. (See the Jerusalem Talmud, *Shevi'it* 6:1: "Your ancestors [observed the commandments related to the land only] while they were not under foreign rule; you must observe them even though you are under foreign rule.")

But this thesis still needs some more clarification: Why should the sanctification imparted by settlement be longer-lasting than the sanctity imparted by conquest? At first glance, the verse "And He will benefit you" does not imply that the consequences of the later sanctification are better than those of the early one. It implies only that at the time of Ezra the sanctification of *Eretz Yisrael* was accomplished by a new means that had not been used earlier (settlement). "Benefit" implies that something new was introduced there.

We are familiar with Maimonides' thesis that the early sanctification of the Temple and Jerusalem was permanent. Maimonides distinguished between the sanctification of the Temple by King Solomon and the sanctification of the land by Joshua. The former was permanent from its inception, whereas the latter was abrogated [by the Babylonian exile, and became permanent only from the time of Ezra]:

Now why is it my contention that as concerns the Sanctuary and Jerusalem, the first sanctification hallowed them for all time to come, whereas the sanctification of the rest of the Land of Israel, which involved the laws of the sabbatical year and tithes and like matters, did not sanctify the land for all time to come? Because the sanctity of the Sanctuary and of Jerusalem derives from the *Shekhinah* [divine presence], which could not be banished…. By contrast, the obligations arising out of the land as concerns the sabbatical year and the tithes had derived from the conquest of the land by the people, and as soon as the land was wrested from them the conquest was nullified. Consequently, the land was exempted by Torah law from tithes and from [the restrictions of] the sabbatical year, for it was no longer deemed the land of Israel. When Ezra, however, came up and sanctified the land, he sanctified it not by conquest but by the act of taking possession. Therefore, every place that was possessed by those who had come up from Babylonia and sanctified by the second sanctification is holy today, even though the land was later wrested from them (Laws of the Temple 6:16).

Here we see that Maimonides drew an analogy between conquest through settlement and the sanctification of the Temple and Jerusalem.

The principle that the sanctity of the First Temple is permanent is based on the presence of the *Shekhinah* there. There is an identification here of sanctity with *Shekhinah*, which distinguishes the sanctity of the Temple from the first sanctification of the land. Even the sanctity imparted by Ezra apparently involves the idea of the *Shekhinah* dwelling wherever the people of Israel settled their land, and it persists in perpetuity. The destruction of the Temple does not lead to an "expulsion" of the *Shekhinah*. "After all, the verse says, 'And I will make waste your sanctuaries' (Lev. 26:31), and the Sages said, 'Even though they are laid waste, their sanctity remains there'" (*Megillah* 28a). What we see here is simple: The idea of man's cleaving to the *Shekhinah* constitutes a firm principle in the Halakhah, whether in relation to times of joy or in relation to the sanctification of the walled-off area of Jerusalem and the Temple.

18. This principle differs from the one common in general philosophy, which claims that God innovated a separate world, and that the entire

existence of the world inheres in its essence as a reality in and of itself. According to this view, only Providence, from the distant reaches of its transcendence, connects the creature with the Creator. Anyone who has fully understood Maimonides can sense that this notion is totally opposed to the aspiration of his lofty soul. His thoughts were dedicated to the vision of the burning bush, the revelation of "I am that I am," and a world that is concentrated and closed off within itself cannot exist. Maimonides never cut off the existence of the world from the existence of God. Such a separation would be the eradication of the world.

"And if it were to be contemplated that He does not exist, then nothing else could exist" (Maimonides, Laws of the Foundations of the Torah 1:2). The world lacks independent existence: It is "open like a porch" to receive its existence from God. If there is a world that exists, its existence "overflows" from the true absolute Existence. There is no existence without God, no reality without the One whose existence is necessary. "All existing things, whether celestial, terrestrial, or belonging to an intermediate class, exist only through His true existence" (Ibid. 1:1). This is the teaching that was given to Moses from the burning bush in the utterance "I am that I am." Maimonides explains:

> God made known to [Moses]…"E-hyeh Asher E-hyeh [I am that I am]." This is a name deriving from the verb hayah [to be], which signifies existence, for the verb hayah indicates the notion that He was…. This makes it clear that He is existent not through existence. This notion may be summarized and interpreted in the following way: the existent that is the existent, or the necessarily existent (Guide of the Perplexed 1:63).

God is the Necessary Existent, and there is no existence without Him, "for everything is attached to Him, in His being" (Laws of the Foundations of the Torah, 2:10).

> One should consider, rather, that just as every existent thing endowed with a form is what it is in virtue of its form – in fact, its being passes away and is abolished when its form passes away – there subsists the very same relation between the Deity and the totality of the remote principles of existence. For the universe exists in virtue of the existence of the Creator, and the latter continually endows it with permanence in virtue of the thing that is spoken of as overflow.

Accordingly, if the nonexistence of the Creator were supposed, all that exists would likewise be nonexistent; and the essence of its remote causes, of its ultimate effects, would be abolished. In this respect it is said of Him that He is the ultimate form and the form of forms; that is, He is that upon which the existence and stability of every form in the world ultimately reposes and by which they are constituted.... Because of this notion, God is called in our language *Hei ha-Olamim* [the Living of the Worlds], meaning the He is the life of the world (*Guide* 1:69).

Similarly, when Maimonides speaks about the nonphysical action that he calls "overflow," he expresses this idea as follows:

Similarly with regard to the Creator, may His name be sublime; inasmuch as it has been demonstrated that He is not a body and it has been established that the universe is an act of His and that He is its efficient cause – as we have explained and shall explain – it has been said that the world derives from the overflow of God, and that He has caused to overflow to it everything in it that is produced in time. In the same way it is said that He caused His knowledge to overflow to the prophets. The meaning of all this is that these actions are the action of one who is not a body. And it is His action that is called overflow. This term, I mean "overflow," is sometimes also applied in Hebrew to God, may He be exalted, with a view to likening him to an overflowing spring of water, as we have mentioned.... As for our statement that the books of the prophets likewise apply figuratively the notion of overflow to the action of the Deity, a case in point is the dictum "They have forsaken me, the fountain of living waters" (Jer. 2:13), which refers to the overflow of life, that is, of being, which without any doubt is life. The dictum "For with You is the fountain of life" (Ps. 36:10) similarly signifies the overflow of being. In the same way the remaining portion of this verse, "In Your light do we see light" (Ps. 36:10), has the selfsame meaning, namely, that through the overflow of the intellect that has overflowed from You, we intellectually cognize, and consequently we receive correct guidance, we draw inferences, and we apprehend the intellect (*Guide of the Perplexed* II:12).

The first fundamental principle is to believe in the existence of the Creator...that He is the cause of all existence. Everything has its existence in Him, and exists through Him (*Commentary to the Mishnah, Sanhedrin*, introduction to *Perek Helek* [chap. 10]).

Maimonides understands the existence of the world not only as caused by God but also as rooted in Him. A world whose existence was separated from God would return to chaos. The world in and of itself does not exist at all; only those who cleave to God enjoy real existence.

19. The Tannaim of the Jerusalem Talmud (*Sukkah* 3:11) were divided on this commandment: Is the verse referring to the obligation of rejoicing when bringing the *shelamim* [peace-offering] or rejoicing when taking the *lulav*? The Babylonian Talmud took it for granted that the verse refers to taking the *lulav*, which is performed in the Temple for seven days – a biblical commandment, as is explained in the Mishnah (*Sukkah* 3:12, *Rosh Hashanah* 4:3). This is how the medieval commentaries interpreted the law as well. According to the opinion in the Jerusalem Talmud that the verse refers to rejoicing when bringing the peace-offering, taking the *lulav* in the Temple all seven days is a commandment established only by the Sages.

Taking the *lulav* in the Temple all seven days actually represented the *realization* (*kiyyum*) of the commandment of being joyous, achieved through taking the *lulav*, an act which constitutes the *performance* of the commandment (*ma'aseh ha-mitzvah*). Man is required to rejoice before God by taking the four species, as the verse formulated this commandment using the word "rejoice" ["and you shall rejoice"]. This sort of joy is different from the holiday joy of festivals generally. When the Temple exists, the *kiyyum* of the commandment of rejoicing on the festivals depends on eating of the sacrifices, but on Sukkot there is a special commandment of rejoicing linked with taking the *lulav*, in addition to the general commandment of holiday rejoicing. The Jerusalem Talmud uses the expression "the rejoicing through the use of the *lulav*," and Maimonides too, in his listing of the commandments, wrote, "to take the *lulav* and to rejoice with it before God on the seven days of the festival" (*Book of the Commandments*, positive commandment 169). Actually, the obligation of rejoicing when performing the ceremony of the drawing of water was also based on this verse. This is what Maimonides did in his *Mishneh Torah* (Laws of the *Lulav* 8:12). He did not cite the verse, "And you shall draw water with joy from the springs of salvation," as explained in *Sukkah* 48b, but instead used the verse, "And you shall rejoice before the Lord your God for seven days" (Lev. 23:40). These are his words: "Even though each of the festivals entails an obligation to rejoice, on the festival of Sukkot there was extra rejoicing in the Temple, as it says, 'And you shall rejoice before the Lord your God for seven days.'" The basic postulate that the obligation of rejoicing is stated in this verse, and that the taking of the *lulav* is only a means that makes it possible to realize the obligation of rejoicing on the festival, is supported by the words of Maimonides. The obligation of rejoicing with the drawing of water also stems from this commandment, which includes a rejoicing that is embodied in two different acts – the taking of the *lulav* and the drawing of water for the sacrificial libation.

The essence of the obligation of rejoicing is rejoicing before God in the Temple. While the general rejoicing of the festivals is fulfilled through bodily enjoyment – eating and drinking – the rejoicing characteristic of Sukkot is expressed by praising and giving thanks to God. The taking of the *lulav* as well, not only in the Temple but also outside it, on the first day of the holiday involves praising God: "Then all the trees of the forest will sing before God" (see the Tosafot commentary on *Sukkah* 37b, s.v. *be-hodu*). The obligatory wavings of the *lulav* during the recitation of the *Hallel* prayer are, in the opinion of many medieval interpreters, an integral part of the commandment of taking the *lulav*. Even those interpreters who claim that it is obligatory to wave the *lulav* at the time of taking it [and not only during the *Hallel*] (see the Tosafot cited above) agree that waving the *lulav* is equivalent to praising God, as is explained in the Babylonian Talmud, *Sukkah* 37b:

> One extends and brings back the *lulav* in all four directions for the One who possesses the four winds; one lifts up and brings down the *lulav* for the One who possesses the heavens and the earth.

Similarly, the commandment of rejoicing in the drawing of water is fulfilled through songs of praise to God, as explained in the Mishnah quoted above, and in Maimonides' *Mishneh Torah*, toward the end of Laws of the *Lulav* [8:12–14]. On Sukkot there is a special commandment of rejoicing in the Temple, a commandment whose goal is to stand before God and cleave to Him. We know from the tales of our sages that the enthusiasm of pious men and men of good deeds would reach a supreme degree on Sukkot. Dancing, singing, juggling with flaming torches, and the like are expressions of sublime divine ecstasy.

Even in the general holiday rejoicing, despite its embodiment in the form of bodily pleasure, there is ensconced a *kiyyum* of rejoicing in the heart, a spiritual act. What expresses the essence of the rejoicing of the heart? The feeling of God's presence and of one's cleaving to Him. The Halakhah contains the simple equation: rejoicing = standing before God. Man is joyous when he stands before God, and when he removes himself from Him, his joy is over. In a word, the *kiyyum* of the commandment of rejoicing on the festivals is rooted in the experience of becoming joined with God, not in the physical act of eating and drinking; this is only the technique for fulfilling the commandment, not the fulfillment itself. Evidence for this view may be found in Nahmanides' remarks in his glosses on Maimonides' *Book of the Commandments*, Root 1, that the *Hallel* said on festivals is a biblical requirement that takes effect together with the commandment of rejoicing. Despite the fact that there is no rejoicing without the eating of the peace offering at the time when the Temple exists in Jerusalem, nor is there eating of nonsacrificial meat and drinking wine outside the Temple, we see that the essence of the fulfillment of the commandment is nevertheless the act of coming closer to God through praise and thanksgiving.

The essence of the assumption that the Halakhah equates rejoicing with standing before God is based on the Babylonian Talmud, *Mo'ed Katan* 10b:

> A mourner does not observe mourning on a festival, as it is said, "And you shall rejoice on your festivals" (Deut. 16:14). If mourning began before the start of the festival, then the arrival of the positive commandment for the community [i.e., rejoicing] outweighs the positive commandment for the individual [i.e., mourning]; and if the mourning began during the festival, the arrival of the positive commandment for the individual would not outweigh the positive commandment for the community.

At first glance it would seem that this passage needs an explanation: Why should one not fulfill both commandments, that of mourning and that of rejoicing on the festival, at the same time? After all, a mourner is permitted to eat meat and drink wine, and where does it say that it is forbidden on a festival to refrain from bathing, anointing oneself, greeting people, and the like? However, this question does not require deep examination. The mutual contradiction between mourning and rejoicing does not involve the behavioral details of mourning and rejoicing. These outward acts do not contradict one another and could easily be accommodated together. The contradiction involves the *kiyyum* of the commandments of rejoicing and mourning in their very essence and in the way they take effect. The essence of rejoicing is an inner act, the heart's joy; likewise, the nature of mourning is the inner attitude, the heart's grief. The Torah commanded that the heart's mourning should put on the outward form of refraining from the acts that are forbidden to a mourner, and that the heart's joy should be symbolized by eating of the peace-offering. These acts, however, are only the means through which man achieves the *kiyyum* of the commandments of inner rejoicing or mourning. Obviously, these two [inner feelings] are mutually contradictory, and opposites cannot be attributed to the same subject simultaneously. Therefore, the arrival of the festival cancels mourning.

The Tosafists (*Mo'ed Katan* 23b, s.v. *man de-amar*), ask: "Why does the Sabbath count as one of the seven days of mourning, whereas the festival does not?" This is a problem for most of the medieval authorities, who hold that mourners must observe the mourning rituals in private even on the festival; yet these days do not count as part of the seven days of mourning. In what way is the festival different from the Sabbath?

The approach presented above allows this problem to be solved without any difficulty. Two different halakhic rules are involved. (1) The festival abrogates the *kiyyum* of mourning, and therefore the festival days are not counted toward the seven days of mourning, because the seven days cannot be completed without the *kiyyum* of mourning. (2) The Sabbath cancels some of the mourning behavior, but does not abrogate the *kiyyum* of mourning entirely, and therefore it may be counted as one of the seven days. The justification for this distinction is that it is the *kiyyum* of the commandment of inner rejoicing which prevents the *kiyyum* of the commandment of inner mourning. But the laws curtailing mourning on the Sabbath stem from the obligation to honor and enjoy the Sabbath, as explained in the *She'iltot* (*Hayyei Sarah*, 15), and this commandment does not refer to one's inner feelings. One honors the Sabbath with clean clothes and enjoys it with food and drink. All of one's Sabbath obligations and fulfillment [of the related commandments] are focused on the acts of honoring and enjoying, which are not rooted in a deep inner experience, as is the rejoicing on the festivals. In short, honor and enjoyment are not dependent on a *kiyyum*. Therefore [the commandment of] inner mourning can apply and be realized on the Sabbath, because there is no commandment of rejoicing on that day. For this reason we say that the Sabbath counts as one of the seven days of mourning. (See the Tosafot commentary on the passage mentioned above, and the commentary of the student of R. Yehiel of Paris, published by the Fischel Institute; this idea is expressed explicitly in their comments.)

The upshot of this view is that the mutual contradiction between holiday rejoicing and mourning is rooted in the inner experience associated with them, not in the outer behavior. When we question more deeply and penetrate the core of this halakhic ruling, we find that the primary basis for the cancellation of mourning is to be found in the halakhic essence of the experiences of rejoicing and mourning. The former is the awareness of standing before God; the latter, of exile and separation from Him. Evidence for this view is the fact that the Talmud established that "for the High Priest the entire year is like the festivals" (*Mo'ed Katan* 14b), and most of the medieval authorities (except for Maimonides) state that he may not perform the customs of mourning for the death of his close relatives. The explanation is simple: Since the High Priest "is always in the Temple," and the laws of being in the Temple apply to him even when he is not physically there, he does not perform the customs of mourning, which imply a separation from God. See Maimonides, Laws of the Temple Vessels 5:7 and Laws of Entry to the Temple 1:10, which teach that the High Priest must obey the commandment "he may not tear his clothes" [on the death of a close relative] (Lev. 21:10) even when he is not in the Temple, since he always is under the obligation to stand before God and be in the Temple.

From this standpoint we understand the prohibitions that apply in common to excommunicated persons, persons afflicted with leprosy, and persons in mourning (see the above-mentioned discussion in *Mo'ed Katan* 14b–16a). In essence, a person in mourning is also excommunicated; for excommunication means being separated from God. Death, according to the Halakhah, is the removal of the *Shekhinah* and the elimination of the image of God. "A mourner is required to turn over his bed, as Bar Kappara taught: A likeness of My image [i.e., a human life] gave I to you, and for your sins I have turned it over [i.e., destroyed it]" (*Mo'ed Katan* 15a–b).

Likewise, evidence that the commandment of rejoicing always refers to an inner experience and constitutes a *kiyyum* of the commandment can be found in the fact that many of the Geonim said the *Hasi'enu* prayer [a festive prayer that expresses joy] on the High Holidays, as explained in the commentary of R. Asher at the end of Tractate *Rosh Hashanah*. The reason they did so is that they considered Rosh Hashanah and Yom Kippur to be included among the festivals on which we are commanded to rejoice. At first glance, this view is astonishing: What place does rejoicing have on the High Holidays, on which we do not bring the peace-offerings that express joy? However, according to our explanation that the commandment of rejoicing is realized through an inner experience, there is nothing to wonder at in their view. The consciousness of standing before God also relates to Rosh Hashanah and Yom Kippur. Characteristically, we decide the Halakhah according to Rabban Gamliel's view that the High Holidays put an end to mourning in the same way that the festivals do. This is a proof for the approach of the Geonim.

The reader should not be troubled as to why excommunicated persons and those suffering from leprosy must nevertheless maintain their prohibitions on the festivals. The medieval authorities have already explained that since individuals in these two categories are separated from the community and cannot cause others to rejoice, then even if they were to observe the commandment of rejoicing, their joy would be, with respect to themselves, the *kiyyum* of an individual commandment. Therefore, the festival joy does not outweigh the obligatory practices of the excommunicated and the leprous.

20. As the [unknown] author of *Iggeret ha-Kodesh* [The Letter on Holiness] wrote:

> Intercourse is holy and pure when it takes place in the proper manner, at the proper time, and with the proper attitude. And no one should say that there is anything bad or ugly about intercourse, Heaven forbid, since it is called "knowledge" [in the Scriptures], as it is said, "And Elkanah knew his wife Hannah" (1 Sam. 1:19). And clearly, if there were not great holiness in the matter, intercourse would not be called knowledge. The matter is not as Maimonides thought when he wrote *Guide of the Perplexed*, where he praised Aristotle's statement that the sense of touch is shameful (*Guide* III:8). Heaven forbid, the matter is not as the Greek said (*Iggeret ha-Kodesh*, chap. 2).

In his *Mishneh Torah*, Maimonides wrote:

> It turns out that one who acts this way all his life is worshiping God
> at all times, even when he is engaged in commerce or sexual inter-
> course, because his intention in all things is to satisfy his needs so that
> his body will be perfected for worshiping God (Laws of Character
> Traits 3:3).

Actually, even Maimonides, despite his ascetic tendencies – which were
expressed particularly in his *Guide of the Perplexed*, where he described
the clash between the bodily instincts and the spirit's longing for God
– had a positive attitude to sexual intercourse. He denounced sexual
overindulgence and sexual provocation. He demanded that man uplift
and sanctify his sexual life by stamping it with a halakhic purpose. This
purpose is threefold:

(1) For one's bodily health, as a physiological function.

(2) For procreating, as a social and religious act: "He [God] did not
create it [the world] to be chaos; He created it for [people] to live" (Isa.
45:18; see *Eduyot* 1:13, *Yevamot* 62a). Maimonides said in his *Mishneh
Torah*: "And when he performs intercourse he should do so only to keep
his body healthy and to procreate" (Laws of Character Traits 3:2).

(3) To continue the chain of our historical spiritual tradition and
fulfill the heavenly mission that was assigned to us: "Even though a
man's wife is always permitted to him, it is appropriate for a Torah
scholar to comport himself with *kedushah* [sanctity].... Anyone who
behaves this way will not only sanctify his soul and purify himself and
correct his traits, but if he has children they will be good-looking and
modest, fit for wisdom and piety" (Laws of Character Traits 5:4–5).

The third purpose, to raise wise and moral children, sanctifies
intercourse and raises it to the level of participation in the act of
Creation.

See R. Sa'adyah Ga'on, *Book of Beliefs and Opinions* VI, on human
behavior, and R. Judah Halevi, *Kuzari* III:1–5. His remarks are also in
this spirit.

21. The idea that prophecy is the ultimate human goal is the basis of
the moral teachings of R. Bahya, R. Judah Halevi, and Maimonides. It
is derived from a statement by R. Pinhas ben Ya'ir that is cited in the
Babylonian Talmud, *Sotah* 49b (in some versions) and *Avodah Zarah*

20b, as well as in the Jerusalem Talmud, *Shekalim* 3:3: "Piety leads to the inspiration of the Holy Spirit." The Holy Spirit is the highest rung on the ladder of the elevation of the soul (prudence or scrupulousness bring on the Holy Spirit).

What is the nature of this preparation? Is it a moral, intellectual effort or an emotional arousal, seething with the awe of mysterious love? The issue is a matter of dispute. Maimonides opted for the former, while R. Judah Halevi and Crescas preferred the latter. But this debate does not involve the obligation to prepare oneself for prophecy, the glory and praise of all the luminaries of the nation. The prophet is the supreme individual, radiating light like a star in the distant heavens and turned to for enlightenment by Israelite morality.

According to Maimonides' teachings, the principle of prophecy includes two elements: (1) the prophet's status – man can reach the level of a prophetic personality; (2) the emanation of the prophecy – God causes human beings to prophesy and inspires them with His spirit. In his *Commentary to the Mishnah* Maimonides wrote:

> The sixth fundamental principle is prophecy. One should know that among men are found certain people so gifted and perfected that they can receive pure intellectual form. Their human intellect clings to the Active Intellect, whither it is gloriously raised. These men are the prophets; this is what prophecy is (introduction to *Perek Helek*).

Therefore the seventh principle, concerning Moses' prophecy, is divided into two parts: (1) The greatest prophet was also the wisest of men. He was the choicest of the human race and the symbol of human perfection. His personality rose to the fullest and noblest height of personal completion. (2) His prophecy was the supreme one.

> The seventh fundamental principle is the prophecy of Moses our Teacher. We are to believe that he was the chief of all other prophets before and after him...all of whom were his inferiors. He was the chosen one of all mankind, superior in attaining knowledge of God to any other person who ever lived or will live. He surpassed the normal human condition and attained the angelic.... Returning to our seventh fundamental principle: Moses' prophecy must be distinguished from that of all other prophets in four respects.

The supreme moral mission begins to be fulfilled in the first degree of prophecy (see Maimonides, Laws of the Foundations of the Torah 4:2, and *Guide of the Perplexed* II:45) and is fulfilled ever more completely as the vision ascends from one degree to the next. It reached its goal in the prophecy and personality of Moses our Teacher, and the exalted mission of man's ability to connect with the Heavenly Throne was fulfilled in all its beauty and glory.

In connection with the concept of prophecy as the supreme moral purpose, as well as the obligation of preparing oneself for it, see R. Judah Halevi, *Kuzari* I:95, 103, 109; II:14, 24, 44; III:5, 11, 21, IV:3–4, 12, 16; Maimonides, *Guide of the Perplexed* II:32, 35, 36; III:17, 18, 51, 52; idem, *Eight Chapters* [introduction to his commentary on *Avot*], chap. 5. Also see R. Bahya, *Duties of the Heart*, Gate of Divine Worship, chap. 3.

22. Maimonides explained this as follows:

> And converts who are not familiar with this are obligated to prepare themselves and listen carefully in dread and awe and trembling joy, as on the day that the Torah was given at Mount Sinai. Even great scholars who know the entire Torah are obligated to listen with very great concentration, and those who are unable to hear must concentrate inwardly on this reading, because the Torah established this commandment only for the purpose of strengthening the true religion, and so that one should see oneself as if one had just been commanded to observe it, and is hearing it from the Deity, as the king is a messenger for proclaiming the words of God (Laws of the Festival Offering 3:6).

What Maimonides wrote about the commandment of *Hakhel* [the septennial reading of the Torah in the Temple on Sukkot] also applies to the ordinary public reading of the Torah in the synagogue: "The interpreter [i.e., the official interpreter appointed to translate the Torah reading into Aramaic because most of the people could no longer understand it in Hebrew] may not lean either on the lectern or on a column, but must stand in dread and awe" (Laws of Prayer 12:11). Moreover, the Jerusalem Talmud states: "R. Shemuel son of R. Yitzhak entered a synagogue. He saw somebody stand up and interpret the Torah reading while leaning on the lectern where the Torah was placed. He told him: 'It is forbidden to do this; just as the Torah was given in awe, so it must be treated with awe'" (Jerusalem Talmud, *Megillah* 4:1).

23. Maimonides described it as follows:

> The nature of this matter makes it necessary for someone to whom this additional measure of overflow has come to address a call to people, regardless of whether the call is listened to or not, and even if, as a result thereof, he is subjected to bodily harm. We even find that prophets addressed a call to people until they were killed – the divine overflow moving them and by no means letting them rest and be quiet, even if they met with great misfortunes. For this reason you will find that Jeremiah, peace be on him, explicitly stated that because of the contempt he met with at the hand of the disobedient and unbelieving people who lived in his time, he wished to conceal his prophecy and not address to them a call to the truth that they rejected, but he was not able to do it. He says, "Because the word of the Lord is made a reproach unto me, and a derision, all the day. And if I say, 'I will not make mention of Him, nor speak anymore in His name,' then there is in my heart, as it were, a burning fire, shut up in my bones, and I weary myself to hold it in, but cannot" (Jer. 22:8–9). This is also the meaning of the words of the other prophet, "The Lord God has spoken, who shall not prophesy?" (Amos 3:8). Know this (*Guide of the Perplexed* II:37).

The stychic [spontaneous, dynamic, elemental] force that motivates the prophet to bestow some of the divine overflow on others is marvelously described by R. Judah Halevi:

> Know that he who converses with a prophet experiences spiritualization while listening to his oration. He differs from his own kind in the purity of soul, in a yearning for the [higher] degrees and attachment to the qualities of meekness and purity (*Kuzari* 1:103).

❧ Index of Biblical and Rabbinic Sources

ಎ Index of Topics and Names

❧ Acknowledgements

We thank the following publishers for their permissions:

American Academy for Jewish Research: From *Moses Maimonides' Epistle to Yemen*, by Abraham S. Halkin, translated by Boaz Cohen, copyright © 1952.

American Jewish Congress: From *Judaism*: "Maimonides on Immortality and the Principles of Judaism," translated by Arnold Jacob Wolf, copyright © 1966.

Feldheim Publishers: From *Duties of the Heart*, translated by Moses Hyamson, copyright © 1970.

Feldheim Publishers: *Mishneh Torah* by Moses Maimonides, translated by Moses Hyamson, copyright © 1981.

Jewish Publication Society of America: From *Tanakh: A New Translation of the Holy Scriptures according to the Traditional Hebrew Text*, copyright © 1985.

Jewish Publication Society of America: From *Three Jewish Philosophers*, Edited by Hans Lewy, Alexander Altmann and Isaak Heinemann, copyright © 1974.

The Soncino Press: *The Zohar*, translated by Harry Sperling and Maurice Simon, copyright © 1931–1934.

University of Chicago Press: From *The Guide of the Perplexed by Moses Maimonides*, translated by Shlomo Pines, copyright © 1963.

Yale University Press: From *The Code of Maimonides Book Eight: The Book of Temple Services*, translated by Mendell Lewittes, copyright © 1957.

Some translations have been slightly modified.